Your Towns and Cit

Manchester
in the Great War

Your Towns and Cities in the Great War

Manchester
in the Great War

Joseph O'Neill

Pen & Sword
MILITARY

First published in Great Britain in 2014 by
PEN & SWORD MILITARY
an imprint of
Pen and Sword Books Ltd
47 Church Street
Barnsley
South Yorkshire S70 2AS

ISBN 978 1 78337 612 4

A CIP record for this book is available from the British Library

Printed and bound in England
by CPI Group (UK) Ltd, Croydon, CR0 4YY

Typeset in Times New Roman

Pen & Sword Books Ltd incorporates the imprints of
Pen & Sword Archaeology, Atlas, Aviation, Battleground, Discovery,
Family History, History, Maritime, Military, Naval, Politics, Railways,
Select, Social History, Transport, True Crime, and Claymore Press,
Frontline Books, Leo Cooper, Praetorian Press, Remember When,
Seaforth Publishing and Wharncliffe.
For a complete list of Pen and Sword titles please contact
Pen and Sword Books Limited
47 Church Street, Barnsley, South Yorkshire, S70 2AS, England
E-mail: enquiries@pen-and-sword.co.uk
Website: www.pen-and-sword.co.uk

Contents

Introduction 6

Chapter One   1914 CARRYING A BOX 8
Chaper Two   1915 KITCHENER'S SMILE 27
Chapter Three 1916 HIGH HOPES AND HOSTILITY 45
Chapter Four   1917 ENDURANCE 61
Chapter Five   1918 THE END 75

Index 95

Introduction

Real heroism is often hidden in the mundane. A single act of courage may save a life but only protracted self-sacrifice can change the world. Sometimes the most heroic act is simply the next thing you have to do. It is impossible to encounter the everyday lives of Mancunians during the Great War without incredulity and awe.

Who were these people, capable of such unremitting toil? How did they endure years of hunger, exhaustion and hardship with such stoicism? How did they withstand the appalling physical and psychological pressure, which met them every morning when they opened their eyes and gripped them even in their few hours of sleep? How did they keep going when so many of their loved ones were exposed to the ever-present threat of death; when the postman was a harbinger of death, when the newspapers told of nothing but death, when death stalked them in their places of work, when the maimed and disfigured who had felt death's breath on their faces stood on every street? How was it possible for these people who had so little to give so much in sweat-stained pennies and halfpennies, earned through endless hours of drudgery, and to continue to give far beyond the demands of generosity?

Of course, it is possible to dismiss these qualities simply by claiming that these people were the products of a different age. Certainly, they were not afflicted by our overweening sense of entitlement, our querulous and litigious conviction that we have an absolute right to a perfect life or that an ubiquitous state is obliged to assuage every inconvenience and compensate for every mishap. True, their perception of Britain had not been poisoned by generations of pusillanimous politicians who believe in nothing and are prepared to stand up for nothing.

On the contrary, the Mancunians of the Great War prided themselves on their independence and ability to provide for themselves and their families by their own resources. They cherished a fierce pride in their city and an instinctive patriotism, which we have since been taught to despise as nothing but the ideology of cynical ruling class. Unfashionable as it is to say, the evidence is incontrovertible: the Great War generation was motivated by municipal pride and love of country, which produced the intense communal instinct that made daily acts of heroism possible.

Venality and self-serving hypocrisy are also part of Manchester's Great War story: idealism would not be idealism if all were idealistic. But this does not diminish the fundamental decency of the working-class people who drove the city's war effort. The comradeship that made the Pals' Battalions so popular was born on the shop floors and in weaving sheds, and in the terraced streets and pubs, long before it found its ultimate expression on the banks of the Somme. The burning sense of 'fair play', the generosity and instinctive compassion for those in need, the resentment of injustice and privilege, the self-reliance and self-respect that characterised working-class communities made the prodigious achievements of the war years possible.

Now more than ever we need to celebrate these achievements and draw inspiration from them. A recent report on the continued educational failure of white working-class children claims that the educational establishment, in its obsession with multiculturalism,

Officers Mess staff belonging to the 13th Manchesters, photographed on 25 November 1914.

has in effect air-brushed British working-class culture and its achievements out of existence, while at the same time systematically undermining several of its central tenets such as patriotism and self-reliance. Britain's white working-class children have been subjected to a process of deculturation, which has cut them off from their roots and undermined that sense of self-worth, without which their forebears would have been incapable of the sacrifices which brought the Great War to a successful conclusion.

Though the war did not create these working-class qualities, it transformed them, raising them to a higher level. The relentless drudgery of those who toiled in factories and workshops was inspired by a love of sons and brothers on the front line. Mancunians' acceptance of affliction for love of their countrymen, is as uplifting as any act of heroism occasioned by the war. As one who spent his life with the poor, and was not given to sentimentalising them, put it, 'The mothers in these homes bear their burdens ungrudgingly, knowing that they are doing their bit in the service of the nation.' Their efforts restore our belief in human nature and are something we should be proud of.

Chapter One

1914 Carrying a Box

'It was the very happiest day of my life.'

THE STULTIFYING HEAT of the July day was killing prize beasts at the Royal Agricultural Show where cattle fell dead in great stolid mounds. In Manchester the gritty haze that swathed the city simmered under the merciless sun. Then at 3.30 pm, with the suddenness of an eclipse, darkness fell. Nature seemed to hold its breath. Passengers on the upper deck of the 53 open top tram, jangling along Great Western Street, began to stir. A shaft of lightning cleft the sky and struck the car, showering the passengers with sparks and lighting up their terrified faces with a harsh glare that blinded many of them. Simultaneously, tramway switches burst into flames and the heavens opened, pouring forth rain that fell in great swirling torrents accompanied by resounding booms of thunder. The lightning destroyed four houses in Pendleton and threatened to smash the great glass dome of the Royal Exchange. 'It seemed for a moment,' said one passenger, 'that we should all be killed.'

The tram was travelling towards Manchester, a city of 714,313 souls, the heart of the greatest textile industry the world had ever known and the centre of a conurbation thirty miles in radius, containing more human beings than any area of similar size anywhere in the world. Though no longer primarily an industrial town and now a market for a vast number of different goods manufactured in surrounding Lancashire, the city remained swathed in a perpetual thundercloud, a noxious vapour of industrial exhalations.

This poisonous breath was one of the reasons why life expectancy in the city was below the national average and Manchester men generally did not live beyond their late forties and women only a few years more. At least two in five of the population were unable to afford food, clothing and shelter sufficient to maintain good health and in many districts poverty was as unremarkable as the rain. Very few of the city's workers' homes had an independent water supply or sanitation. The people were obstinate and self-willed with a grim humour that delighted in jests about poverty, illness and death. Yet they had a great capacity to endure hardship, and a fundamental decency. They combined a fierce sense of independence and self-reliance with a combative cussedness that made them good comrades and bad enemies.

As one who grew up in Irk Town, Collyhurst in the years before the Great War described it, the city consisted of 'viaducts cutting through the streets, factories, foundries, storage sheds, forges, workshops, gasometers, clusters of small terraced houses, railway yards, sidings, stables, water towers, and churches', with every road slashed through by black rivers and canals. And noise – incessant, pervasive and ever-present, shaking the walls and making the pavements throb. The smoke of cotton mills and foundries had painted the ochre bricks black. Engineering, iron and steel employed over 55,000 men, the Manchester Docks over 6,000, while 10,000 produced chemicals and explosives. The success of all these was central to Britain's entire war effort. As much as any British city, Manchester became the engine driving the machinery of war to ultimate victory.

Hard as life was, for the unskilled it was getting harder. The life of Tom Haddock, born in 1899 within the sound of the trains at London Road Station, was fairly typical. Tom was one of ten children – all born in different houses as his family regularly 'did a moonlight'. He remembers Ancoats as a 'dirty, lousy 'ole and very poor'. None of the houses he grew up in had gas, electricity or running water; the family washed at the pump in the yard and used communal toilets. Most of Tom's neighbours were in unskilled jobs: working on the railways as porters or engine cleaners and goods yard labourers, existing on less than a pound a week. Like most Ancoats children, Tom was undernourished and went to school in a smock and bare feet. When he heard the call to arms, like so many others, 'he felt that little shiver run up the back and you know you have got to do something'.

But the city also had a thriving middle class, grown affluent and confident on Manchester's industry, commerce and trade. Among the lower middle class, commerce was the biggest employer, providing work for one in ten of the population, including 16,000 merchants and agents and 22,000 commercial clerks. The Manchester Docks, linked to Liverpool by the Manchester Ship Canal, made the land-locked city an international marine port and a centre of commerce and warehousing. It was this distinctive combination of trade and industry that gave the city its unique character.

Deansgate's opulent shops catered for all the consumer whims of a flourishing middle class conscious of its status and physically separate from the working class. Bound by their common interest in lacrosse, hockey and cricket, many middle class men also shared a passion for the Territorial Army and devoted their Saturdays to drilling at Stretford Road barracks. The most ambitious of these aspired to an abode in Wilmslow or Alderley Edge, from which the 8.05 and the 8.32 carried the new aristocracy of wealth to their places of work. Engineering companies such as Mather and Platt and Whitworth

Mather & Platt, one of the city's most prestigious companies. Mark Flynn Postcards

Lancashire Fusiliers, men of a Territorial battalion on a route march. They came from communities north and west of Manchester and Salford. Taylor Library

were internationally respected enterprises of enormous prestige. Manchester Grammar School, Chetham's, William Hulme and Victoria University prepared them for the professions and introduced many of them to the military ethos through their Officers Training Corps. Many of the first to go to war August 1914 were from this social milieu. Their patriotism was intense and their entitlement to form the officer elite of the new army was unquestioned. In peacetime they were leaders of the city's economic, social and political life and in war they presumed that they would be at the forefront of the national cause.

During the last days of peace Lancashire was taking on Surrey at Old Trafford and Hobbs and Hayward were striking for cover and slip. The crowd, enjoying this exemplary display of batting in the July sunshine, gave little thought to the conference of health professionals at Leeds University pondering the curse of consumption, which culled the poor and ill-housed; they were untroubled by the rancour that saw a staggering forty million days lost to industrial disputes in 1912; they were indifferent to the 500

engineers locked out in Accrington and the two hundred Ashton coal miners who were in court, charged with absenting themselves from work without leave after one of their colleagues was killed. They were only vaguely aware of the dock strike, which saw troops on the streets of Liverpool and gunboats in the Mersey and the years of industrial conflict that had raged since 1911 were a distant memory.

In the city's parks 2,000 slum children were also untroubled. Though many were shoeless, they were enjoying their traditional summer outing, courtesy of the readers of a local newspaper.

Though page eight of the *Manchester Evening News* told of the removal of the bodies of the assassinated Archduke and his wife – whose murder would spark a chain of events leading to the outbreak of war – to Vienna, Manchester was concerned mainly with the cotton depression. Many mills were closed and trade prospects were grim. The news from Dublin, where British soldiers fired on civilians, killing three and wounding eighty, including many women and children, was more troubling: people feared civil war in Ireland. On Friday, 31 July the London and Manchester stock exchanges both closed. Something was afoot: the Special Reserve was called up, while Manchester's suburban

Middleton companies of 1/6 Battalion, Lancashire Fusiliers, marching to war from their drill hall on Manchester New Road in August 1914. Moonraker Press, Lancs.

grocers experienced an unprecedented surge in demand. Saturday, 1 August was the busiest day many could remember: frantic housewives bought up flour, bacon and sugar for fear of imminent shortages and price hikes.

Monday, 3 August was a bank holiday and though the forecast was good a storm broke over the city and rain pounded down on those in the Cathedral, offering prayers for peace as the Dean, Edmund Know, told the congregation the continental conflict was not Britain's concern. Across the city in St Francis's monastery, Gorton, his Catholic counterpart, Bishop Casartelli, expressed his hope that 'the nation would not proceed to extremities'. Local trade unions convened a protest meeting in Alexandra Park and asserted that Britain should not 'be dragged into war'. But the feeling in the pubs and workshops was that it was high time Germany was taught a lesson, an opinion echoed in a letter to a local newspaper. The writer welcomed the war as an opportunity to 'smash up the German fleet', which 'they should never have been allowed to build or own'.

As Tuesday, 4 August dawned and Reservists rushed to their barracks while the Territorials awaited their orders, Germany declared war on France and Britain issued an ultimatum, due to expire at midnight: if the Germans do not withdraw from Belgium, Britain will declare war.

As darkness fell the streets and trams were full as people made their way to the city centre, gathering in Shudehill for the special editions of the *Manchester Evening News* that appeared every few hours. The 9.30 pm edition reported no developments. The crowd dispersed and most made their way home, while others cheered the naval reservists departing from London Road Station.

Across the city, C. P. Scott, the eminent editor of the *Manchester Guardian*, told a meeting of businessmen that, 'If we rush into a war...it will be both a crime and ruinous madness in which we risk everything of which we are proud and in which we stand to gain nothing.' The eminent eugenicist, Dr C.W. Saleeby, told the Manchester Statistical Society that war would wipe out 'the physically and morally best of the nation's manhood, slaughtering the best and strongest and sacrificing the future of the race'.

When the news finally broke there was no cheering, no patriotic songs, no 'mafficking'. Manchester heard the declaration of war with characteristic resignation and a mood, described by a local journalist, as 'quiet and intense seriousness'. The declaration was a release from uncertainty. 15-year-old Joe Fagan did not feel anything political, except that 'poor little Belgium had been invaded.' Feelings were similar in nearby Salford, where Robert Roberts remembers 'no great burst of patriotic fervour. Little groups, men and women together, stood talking earnestly in the shop or at the street corner, stunned a little by the enormity of events.'

Already Manchester men were on their way to the front. Among the first to arrive on 7 August was Mike Lally, of the 2 Battalion Manchester Regiment. He went to France as part of the British Expeditionary Force, and was at the fore of the fighting throughout the period of mobile conflict until November 1914, when the war settled down into a stalemate. One of eight children from Cheetham Hill, Mike was a product of St Joseph's Approved School, Longsight, which 'made a man of me ... I thought it was great'. He fought in the first battle of the war, the defence of the Mons-Condé Canal and in the retreat to Le Cateau. Such was the casualty rate in the British ranks that Mike was promoted to lance corporal at the age of twenty. When the tide turned and the Germans were driven back, he fought in the Battle of the Marne, one of the most significant battles in military history, and the First Battle of Ypres.

Among the first to volunteer for foreign service was Alexandre Doig, a graduate of Manchester's Victoria University, a prized electrical engineer of Westinghouse – a world leader in the production of turbines and generators – and a talented footballer who played for Eccles Borough FC.

Ridley Sheldon, an employee of woollen merchants Sparrow Hardwick, was not able to join the 1st City Battalion immediately, as he was on a cycling holiday in the Lake District. On his return he went to his local recruiting office and signed up for four years' foreign active service. Years later he vividly remembered it as 'one of the very happiest days of my life'. At 8.15 am the next morning, his belongings wrapped in newspaper, he and his fellow volunteers gathered at the drill hall on Stretford Road and marched to Victoria Station. Though they cut a distinctly unmilitary spectacle, those gathered to watch their progress cheered them enthusiastically.

Men seeking to enlist gathered outside the Town Hall, 1 September, 1914. Taylor Library

Jack (John Clarke) Morten of 7th Manchesters was immediately caught up in the war. A manufacturer's agent, based in Piccadilly, he mobilized at his Burlington Street barracks on 4 August and five weeks later he was on his way to Egypt. First he spent a few weeks training at Hollingworth Camp, Littleborough. Among his new comrades was 16-year-old Joe Horgan, still living in the 'one-room house' he was born in on Oldham Road. When war broke out he was employed as an errand boy for outfitters Dobbs & Son in Piccadilly, working nine to five – known as 'short hours' – for a wage of five shillings a week. For Joe the war was 'a grand opportunity to join the army and see the world'. Enlisting went some way to making up for his disappointment at not being able to join the Scouts because he could not afford the uniform. The first perk of joining the army was the boots he received, of which he was inordinately proud.

Novice soldiers drilled in Heaton Park, White City, Belle Vue and the Exhibition Hall. The Territorials eventually set up training camp at Hollingworth Lake. Rows of white tents ran the full sweep of the valley, from beside the lake to its steep rise towards Blackstone Edge. After weekdays drilling and marching, the recruits delighted in telling their friends and families who visited at the weekend of their ample rations which

Heaton Camp, 11 September, 1914. Left to right: RQMS Walker; Major Singleton; Lieutenant Colonel Crawford and Arthur Taylor of the Raising Committee. Taylor Library

included 1½lb of both meat and bread and 4oz of bacon. Over the weekend of 24 and 25 August no less than 51,000 visitors thronged to Hollingworth Lake.

Within days of the declaration of war, Manchester appeared entirely given over to fighting the Germans. Territorials with fixed bayonets marched to guard duty. Manchester's large Irish community learnt that Nationalist MPs had agreed to suspend Home Rule agitation – and their leader, John Redmond, called on nationalists to fight for the integrity of small nations like Belgium while the Unionists, who had armed themselves against Home Rule, swore that the Ulster Volunteer Force would be in the forefront of the fight against Prussian militarism.

The city was caught up in a collective compulsion to be part of it. Special constables – men too old, medically unfit for the army or involved in key war work – were everywhere drilling in their waistcoats and shirt sleeves. When the first batch of thirty-nine were sworn in at the Manchester County Police Court, Mr R. A. Arbitrage, chairman of the bench, thanked them for offering their services 'at a time when all men should be doing something for their country'. The Watch Committee aimed to recruit 5,000 specials; by 11 September 2,500 were already training and by Christmas the full quota had joined up to form a civic guard trained to drill and shoot. They took on crucial

The Lord Mayor, Sir Daniel McCabe, swearing in recruits to a Territorial battalion raised in Manchester in early 1915. Taylor Library

responsibilities, including guarding key installations, escorting prisoners and crowd control.

As well as giving time, people demonstrated staggering generosity. By the end of 1914, £165,568 had been subscribed to various war funds – in addition to an unspecified amount contributed to a range of special appeals such as the relief of refugees. (At this time the average weekly wage was less than £1.) Not only were several thousand volunteers giving their time to organisations such as the Red Cross and the Relief Committees but numerous private homes were lent and furnished at the owners' expense for the reception of wounded soldiers and refugees. The public donated everything from motor cars and household goods to clothing and books. Quite apart from this there was an enormous amount of private endeavour by individuals who organized benefits, concerts, bazaars, whist drives and social gatherings in order to raise funds. Many firms were paying half or in some cases the full wages of employees who had volunteered. Working people had contributed out of all proportion to their income – Corporation employees alone had given £10,000.

Kitchener, however, knew that no amount of money could substitute for the men needed to fight the war. A military hero lionised for his exploits in the Sudan and the Boer War, the newly appointed Secretary for War believed Britain needed an entirely new army of half a million volunteers and launched a campaign to raise them. Kitchener's accusatory finger pointed out from every pub window, wall and billboard, demanding that every man join the 100,000 required immediately for the regular army. Within days soldiers seemed to be everywhere: they had already requisitioned and were moving into the School of Technology, the Municipal Secondary School for Boys on Whitworth Street and the university residences of Dalton Hall and Hulme Hall.

In order to increase recruitment, Edward Stanley, Earl of Derby, Lancashire's foremost landed aristocrat, launched the first 'Pals Battalion' in Liverpool. The idea was that volunteers served with men of their own community or occupational group. The territorial force already drew on the camaraderie of the locality as it had, from its inception in 1908, been drawn from their local communities, though many also had a distinctive social character. For instance, 6 Manchesters, recruited mainly from the area around its barracks in Hulme, consisted of middle class commercial, financial, legal and managerial types.

Fired with civic rivalry, Manchester's elite was determined not to be outdone by Liverpool: as soon as Lord Derby invited recruits for the first Manchester Pals' Battalion – known as the Manchester Clerks' and Warehousemen's Battalion – local employers immediately offered the money to equip it.

Yet it was often the volunteers themselves who were making the greatest financial sacrifice. A corporal's pay was only 1/- a day, while a sergeant earned only 3/3 a day.

Some early recruits to a battalion of the Manchester Regiment in tented accommodation.
Taylor Library

The allowance for married men was initially derisory – 1/1 a day for the wife of a corporal and 2d a day for boys under 14 and girls under 16. To encourage rapid recruitment to the Pals' Battalion, Manchester's leading merchants and employers offered all who volunteered within a fortnight four weeks' full pay, re-employment upon discharge and half pay to the wives of married men during their husbands' military service. Manchester City Corporation gave all its employees in the Reserves and the Territorials half pay for the duration, while the Lord Mayor promised that the Education Committee would feed their children while they were away.

The result was beyond anyone's expectations: men clamoured to enlist and a queue snaked a mile along Hyde Road from the Artillery HQ. The recruiting staff were overwhelmed. The numbers surrounding the Town Hall were such that the Albert Hall had to be used as a makeshift recruiting centre and extra medical and clerical staff drafted in. In a single day the Lord Mayor, Alderman Daniel McCabe, personally swore in 800 men. It took precisely two days to recruit the entire 1st City Battalion. There was no sign of the fervour abating during September and on 3 September alone 2,151 men enlisted in Manchester, second only to the 3,521 in London. Eventually the city provided fifteen of Kitchener's 134 battalions, more than any other provincial city.

These men and those of the Lancashire Fusiliers, which also numbered many Mancunians, were at the centre of arguably the greatest battle of the war fought on the Somme in 1916.

The flood of recruits peaked in late August and early September when local papers informed readers that the standard of volunteers was consistently high. Most of those rejected were suffering from poor eyesight, varicose veins or chest complaints. So keen were volunteers that even those who were clearly below the minimum height requirement nevertheless presented themselves for examination. One such was Charles Cain, who in addition was only 15. The sergeant who measured him pronounced, 'Four foot eleven' and then asked the clerk, 'What's the lowest height for the British Army?' 'Five foot five,' the clerk replied. The sergeant then picked up a small box, told Charles to stand on it and having measured him again shouted out, 'Five foot five'. When Charles stepped down the sergeant looked at him and said, 'Just one small problem. You will have to carry this box around with you all the time you are in army in case someone

Lancashire Brigade arrives at Amesbury Station en route to Salisbury Plain.
Mark Flynn Postcards

THE LANKCASHIRE BRIGADE ARRIVES

New recruits constructing the training camp in Heaton Park. Tameside Archives

wants to know how tall you are.'

Not all of those who presented themselves at the recruiting offices encountered such ingenious sergeants. Large numbers were actually rejected because of the height qualification. Consequently, Didsbury's Mr D.E. Anderson, of the Manchester Branch of the National Service League, started enrolling men for 'Bob's Bantams', open to men above five feet tall, who would eventually form 8th City Battalion and fight in some of the bloodiest battles of the war.

Albert Edward Cardigan Andrews, one of Charles Cain's comrades in the 4th Battalion, had no concerns about meeting the entry requirement. His grandfather, David

New recruits constructing the training camp in Heaton Park. Tameside Archives

New recruits cooking over a camp fire. Tameside Archives

Andrews, was one of the survivors of the charge of the Light Brigade and his father treasured the great man's spurs as the family's most prized heirloom. When war broke out Albert was working as a storeman for the railway in Ardwick, a job he detested. One of seven children – two died at birth and another at 12-years-old – the war offered release from his cramped home in West Gorton and the tedium of the warehouse. Albert's feelings were perfectly expressed by another early volunteer: 'I couldn't see myself catching the 8.40 every morning ...and all the time my pals were suffering – probably dying somewhere.'

Why this headlong rush to danger by so many? Undoubtedly there were those like Albert for whom the war offered an escape from the grind of monotonous, exhausting and badly paid toil and the tedium of endless routine. For others it was an escape from unemployment. On 18 August there were 14,000 officially unemployed, three times the city norm, and certainly far short of the real figure. Additionally, thousands were on short time. How enticing was the glamour of war, especially when flecked with patriotic ardour and the idealism of self-sacrifice? Looking back on those heady days of early August, many Manchester veterans remember their indignation at the invasion of 'poor little Belgium' and the sense that they were fighting to right a great wrong.

On his re-election as Lord Mayor on 9 November 1914, Daniel McCabe spoke of Manchester's pride as 'a great city of the Empire ready to shoulder a large part of the burden of the war'. He boasted of the city's enormous financial contribution to both the relief of Belgian refugees and the Red Cross. But above all he delighted in the fact that 'Manchester has contributed more men to the army and the navy as a percentage of its population than any other city or town in Britain'.

And there was no doubt that every man was needed. By 14 September the war had begun to assume the form of two entrenched armies, each with its forehead up against the other, trying to push its opponent back. Initially it was the French and British who were driven back, forced to fight a delaying strategy, holding up the German advance at Mons and Le Cateau, but eventually being pushed back to the Marne, where the German progress was finally halted almost in sight of Paris. It was then the turn of the German to retreat to the river Aisne as both sides raced for the sea, trying to capture the Channel ports. The first Battle of Ypres ensured that these vital links with Britain remained in Allied hands. The war then settled down into a murderous deadlock in which each side eyeballed the other across a ribbon of murdered nature that stretched 460 miles from the English Channel to the Swiss Alps. The war had assumed the character which was to make it unlike any other.

The concerns of those back in Manchester were more mundane. The uncertainty of war plunged industry into depression. Major employers – cotton and engineering especially– lost large contracts and in addition to the many men and women who were laid off, others were put on short time. On 13 August 1914 a single Manchester engineering company laid off its entire workforce of 2,000 men. Little business was being done in the city's warehouses and droves of men were sent home early from the sprawling Trafford Park industrial estate. Few goods were going out of Manchester Docks.

Worst affected was the cotton industry. In the early days of the war the threat of the wholesale closure of mills hung over the city, convincing many that hardship was the first fruit of war. As one local paper put it, 'Poverty is beginning to stalk in our midst. We have it on good authority that unless a very great change comes there will scarcely be a cotton mill working in Lancashire within a month.' Railway men too had reason to worry: the government took over the network and normal services were suspended – all the holiday trains to Blackpool were cancelled at a time of year when they were normally packed with holidaymakers.

While the price of cotton on the Manchester Exchange plummeted that of foodstuffs – particularly the staples, flour, butter and bacon and non-perishables such as sugar and tinned foods – soared as panic buying pushed up prices. Hardship led to dissension: the first rumblings of class antagonism found expression in a local newspaper which complained of 'Well-to-Do People's Disgraceful Conduct' in cornering supplies of essential foods.

In October 1914 the accusation that employers were using the war as a pretext for exploiting workers raised its head for the first of many occasions. A Mr Melia complained bitterly to the Manchester Distress Committee that a number of employers were forcing workers to accept reduced wages on the grounds that trade was slack, while simultaneously recruiting additional staff. In a letter to a local newspaper one correspondent denounced the 'unpatriotic and dastardly treatment of their employees' by some local retailers who were forcing their lady assistants to take a cut in their weekly wage down from 10/- to 12/-. Such behaviour proved they were no more than 'filthy mud-wallowing misers', in the words of another correspondent.

This allegation reappeared throughout the war in numerous forms. In December 1914 the Manchester and Salford Trade and Labour Council complained that the callous employers were even exploiting Belgian refugees, seeking 'to get 35/- worth of work out of them for 15/-.'

Writing to the *Manchester Evening News* on 7 August, 'Reno' captured the mood of the city: 'the price of all basic foods is already rising at a time when many people were out of work'. By 11 August it was widely accepted that the rate of unemployment in certain parts of the city had trebled in the previous week. The garment trade, wages in which were notoriously low, was among the worst hit, with many of those still in work reduced to short time. Many of the unemployed were 'entirely without means' and there was a clamour for the local District Committees to provide work schemes.

On 19 August, in response to the uproar, Manchester Corporation announced a work creation scheme that involved the digging of lakes in three municipal parks and a new road from Slade Lane to Cheadle and Gatley at a cost of £172,000. Despite these measures, on 12 September there were still 4,000 men in Manchester unemployed and half that number in Salford. By the autumn the Corporation was devising work schemes for drainage, electricity generation and road improvement.

Though there was less discussion of it, the plight of the lower middle class was as unenviable as that of manual workers. Many clerks found that employers were using the downturn in trade as justification for reducing their wages, many being forced to accept as much as a fifty per cent cut to a wage of £1 a week. Many more were on short time. This decline in both the real value of middle class incomes and their relative value in relation to most manual workers

continued throughout the war and led many to believe that they had paid a disproportionately high price for victory. In particular, shop assistants of both sexes and warehousemen found themselves unemployed in large numbers.

By the onset of winter things began to improve. In November there were only 3,000 unemployed – fewer than at the corresponding time in 1913. Engineers, severely hit in August, were once more employed producing munitions; while the demand for joiners and builders to construct military buildings exceeded the supply. Yet it was not until 1915 that engineers enjoyed full employment. The cotton trade alone seemed to be stagnant.

As industry picked up, more women were drawn into employment. Work outside the home, particularly in the mills, was nothing new to Manchester women. What was new was the extent of it and the opening up of occupations previously the exclusive domain of men. Women played a big part in replacing the city's commercials who had joined up

New recruits in the mess hall. Tameside Archives

and the number of women in traditional women's jobs, such as clothing and domestic service, declined during the war. Many Manchester women moved into war work.

Nothing, however, could replace the limbs of the maimed and the city was always aware of their suffering as hospitals sprang up everywhere and wounded soldiers were seen on every street. By mid-September 1914 the casualties were arriving at Whitworth Street Military Hospital in ever larger numbers. The first group, consisting of 125 men of the Lancashire and Manchester regiments, arrived at Mayfield Station. The authorities had not publicised the event yet a small group of voluble civilians met the train and ensured that the men got a rousing reception.

The presence of large numbers of wounded soldiers brought civilians as near to the reality of war as it is possible for a civilian to get. In Moss Bridge Red Cross and St John's Hospital there was a mock-up of a front line trench, a source of endless fascination and a major fund-raising attraction for visitors who looked with awe and sympathy on the wounded soldiers in their convalescent blue uniforms. Parents told gleeful children that normal schooling would not be resumed in September after the school holidays: the buildings were to be used by the British Red Cross as hospitals for wounded soldiers. Throughout the war the city was a major centre for the treatment of those wounded on the Western Front, with 5,000 men being cared for by the end of November 1914. That month Trafford Hall was converted into a hospital with a thousand beds.

Local Red Cross branches burgeoned during the war and provided many middle class girls with the opportunity to make a practical contribution to the war effort. The Victoria Park branch converted 30 Daisy Bank Road into a military hospital and a centre for training nurses and stretcher bearers. The branch had no funds and therefore no alternative but to appeal for charity. The most charitable givers of all were the professional nurses, who gave their services free and took responsibility for instructing the 'delicately nurtured young ladies who threw away fripperies and attired themselves in cotton prints, and went through a course of knee-aching floor scrubbing followed by spells at the washtub'. Even more amazing was the process by which 'the sister of a distinguished Manchester surgeon was metamorphosised into a hospital cook'. When the neighbours heard of the hospital's work they agreed to feed the patients. In order to encourage public donations, the hospital provided visits for the public and the response was such that it was soon able to plan for expansion, including the building of a new wing.

Wounded soldiers became the focus of a great deal of voluntary work that soon

Whitworth Street, site of the Second Western Military Hospital, and Oxford Road, the route of wounded soldiers to convalescent homes in the south of the city. Mark Flynn Postcards

became a national obsession and touched every strata of society and every age group. Volunteers set about gathering newspapers, books and bookshelves for the men and organizing people to read to them and to wounded Belgians in Flemish and French.

Of course, the plight of wounded soldiers soon affected Mancunians in a more personal way. The list of killed and wounded became a grim fixture in the local papers. The first list of 'Local Casualties: Wounded Men from the Manchester Regiment' appeared in the *Manchester Evening News* on 5 September and subsequently became grim compulsive reading. As one diarist said, 'it is impossible to read it without finding at least one son of a friend or neighbour'. From 7 September names were listed under three headings: Killed, Wounded and Missing. Relations of the latter, however, had reason to be hopeful, especially after J.A.F. Aspinall, general manager of the Yorkshire and Lancashire Railway Company, was repatriated from Germany in September. He told the local papers that he had details of Manchester soldiers he had met in his PoW camp, all of whom had been posted missing and presumed dead.

The story of Mrs Lucas of Shrewsbury Street, Old Trafford, also gave hope to all of those whose husbands were unaccounted for. The War Office informed her in September that her husband, a postman before the war, had been killed in action. Two months later she received a postcard from him assuring her that he was PoW. The same surprise relieved the desolation of Lance Corporal J. Dale's family when they received news from him in their Higher Broughton home.

But for most there was no reprieve from the buff envelope stamped with the War Office crest. The loss of each man was a family tragedy and a defining point in the lives of those who mourned him. The lists of the dead reminded those not directly affected of the nearness of death, only as far away as the next postal delivery. A Middleton man remembers seeing the local postman sitting on the kerb crying and wiping his tears with a great red and white handkerchief. He had been delivering the War Office letters to the nearby cottages. A white-faced, clogged and shawled old lady held his hand. Up and down the city in churches where the men had worshipped memorial services were a daily occurrence.

Describing her childhood in wartime Manchester, when her father was at the front, Mary Jordan captures this pervasive fear. 'Mam always seemed to be upset but I could not understand why. "What was it, war?" I kept asking myself, "and why had my dad to go away?" Mam used to read the letters to Joe [Mary's brother] and I; quite often I would find her reading them to herself when I came in, then she would hurriedly push them into her pinny pocket.'

Emma Pollitt, looking back on her childhood in the Deansgate area of Manchester, remembers that her grandmother, Mrs Derbyshire, suffered a stroke, which the doctors attributed directly to worry about her son, Fred, who was serving at the front. When talking of him her constant refrain was, 'So far away and so long'. She worried about him not having enough to eat and sent him egg and bacon pies through the post.

The first Christmas of the war was like none in living memory. The economic situation was improving, which was unusual for that time of year, but the 50,000 Mancunians who had joined the armed services were away from home. At the beginning of December, Mr T. Johnson, superintendent of Charter Street Ragged School – a major philanthropic institution in Angel Meadow, the poorest part of the city – made his annual appealed for dolls, trumpets and other toys, enough to ensure that each of the 500 children they fed on Christmas Day received a gift.

One local newspaper berated the scaremongers for suggesting that shortage would force up food prices and assured its readers that they were lower than normal 'in some respects'. There was, admittedly, none of the traditional game and fowl, imported from Germany and Austria in pre-war days, but production in Ireland and Scotland made up the shortfall. True, there was a fish famine – at Shudelhill lemon sole was fetching twice the price of turkey per pound. Yet, although there were no Jaffa oranges, bananas were plentiful as half the crop previously went to Germany and there was an abundance of apples. Tenerife tomatoes, however, were expensive.

As the festive season approached one observer remarked that 'there never was a time when the principal centres of Manchester shopping activity looked less like Christmas than the present moment. The elegantly dressed windows, designed to entice the public, are absent and instead everything speaks of the war – most of all the shop displays, which are full of presents ranging from woollen socks to binoculars advertised as suitable for soldiers. It seems that toy soldiers, military aircraft and destroyers are the only gifts available for boys and the once ubiquitous German toys are nowhere to be found. In homes and offices there was little holly or mistletoe to be seen.'

The best gift of all went to the beleaguered cotton workers: the government placed an order for a million yards of cotton khaki with the promise that if it proved successful much more would be needed.

Chapter Two

1915: Kitchener's Smile

'Manchester's army is Manchester.'

'Germans machine gun 450 civilians in the village of Tamines!'
'Child raped and murdered in front of her parents'
'Germans hang priests.'

FROM THE OPENING days of the war the government doled out so little war news that Manchester newspapers latched onto these and other atrocity stories of fleeing refugees in a desperate attempt to get news of the conflict. But, as the weeks passed, the newspapers made it clear there was no sign of an early end to the war and thus helped the population to come to terms with the prospect of a lengthy conflict that would encroach more and more on the lives of civilians.

Anti-German feelings in Manchester were further aroused in October 1914 with the arrival of fifty Belgian refugees, who were housed in Longford Hall, Stretford. 'Simple, inoffensive peasant folks, each carrying all his worldly possessions in a small bundle to which he clung tenaciously', their appearance aroused the compassion of the crowds who greeted them at Exchange Station. One spectator elicited a loud cheer when he called out, 'Bravo les Belges!'. By August 1915 there were 3,000 in the city and Manchester took them to its heart. Mr H. M. Worthington put Sale Hall at their disposal as accommodation and a local fund-raising committee collected over £14,000 through donation boxes on the trams. In addition, the Manchester branch of the Serbian Relief Fund raised £6,700.

Belgian refugees were not the only ones who brought the realities of war to the city. Though Manchester was not a conventional port, it was not long before the predations of the war at sea struck the city. A German U-Boat sank the *Manchester Commerce* in the North Channel the day after it left Manchester on 25 October 1914, with the loss of fourteen crew. On 2 March 1915 the city celebrated a naval triumph: John William Ball, captain of the steamer *Thordis*, out of Manchester, rammed and sank a German U-boat in the English Channel – the first occasion a merchantman had sunk an enemy submarine. The crew won not only the acclaim of the nation but were also entitled to a reward of £1,000 from the government, £500 from a shipping newspaper and several smaller prizes. Later that month the Captain, now a lieutenant of the Naval Reserve and proudly displaying his DSC, was the guest of honour at the Manchester Rotary Club, where he recounted his exploits.

The war at sea was also a major factor in turning the people against the beleaguered foreigners in their midst. On the outbreak of war the Chief Constable, Robert Peacock, announced that every 'alien enemy'—German and Austrian – must register forthwith at the Town Hall or face 'severe penalties'. They must not change their address or employment or travel more than five miles from home without his permission. Nor were they allowed to own petrol or pigeons. This had a significant impact as Manchester was, outside London, the chief centre in England for continental immigrants, with over 2,000 Germans living in the city and several hundred in Salford, working mainly as pork butchers, waiters, barbers, hoteliers and musicians. There were also a number of Hungarians and 3,000 Turks, almost all men involved in the shipping business; practically every important commercial business in England had a branch in Manchester. Turks were not required to register as aliens until November when their worst fears were realised and Britain declared war on their country.

In early September 1914 Germans of military age were arrested, many taken from their homes at the dead of night. By 11 September 1914, 300 had been arrested, with a view to exchanging them for Britons in enemy hands. One German, Max Shoeke, unwisely concealed unregistered firearms in his Old Trafford home and was consequently sentenced to two months' hard labour.

It was the following month that Manchester's aliens felt the full effects of the war. Between 21 and 23 October, 600 men between the ages of 17 and 45, were arrested. Housed in police cells overnight, they were then ferried in chains to Exchange Station on their way to Lancaster. Though spectators at the station generally expressed approval, some were moved by the tearful separations they saw. One commented, 'You don't like to see a young woman crying', but then added, 'Think of the British mothers, wives and sisters whose young ones have been killed.' The English wives and children of many of those interned had no means of support and found themselves plunged into hardship and in some cases destitution, while their men folk spent the bulk of the war in Knockaloe Camp on the Isle of Man.

The great bulk of aliens, however, including those with children in the British forces, were deemed harmless and allowed to remain at liberty or, if they chose, return to Germany.

The city's Greeks were in a precarious position as Greece remained neutral until 1917. On 10 March, a meeting of Manchester Greeks at the Midland Hotel sent a telegram to the Greek President urging 'immediate armed co-operation with the Allies'.

So far, so cordial. Then a series of events in 1915 made aliens the object of intense hatred. High among these were German attacks on civilians in the south and east of England. Though Manchester was untouched by Zeppelin raids, they nevertheless had a profound effect on the city, providing incontrovertible proof that the Germans were barbarians who murdered women and children without compunction. The air raids created a pervasive sense of vulnerability far beyond their capacity to inflict damage.

Though the first attack on British soil took place in November 1914 it was not until 16 December, with the naval bombardment of Hartlepool, that Britain suffered her first civilian casualties. The 150 shells that rained down on the coastal town, killing ninety-seven men, women and children and maiming 466, attracted enormous coverage in the Manchester newspapers and signalled the end of any illusion that civilians had about being immune from sudden death by enemy action.

Hartlepool bomb damage.

The sinking of the *Lusitania* off the coast of County Cork with the loss of 1,906 British and American lives on 7 May was also extensively reported in local newspapers and was met with outrage throughout the city. It led to an immediate surge in recruitment and an outbreak of anti-German attacks, mainly on shops and business owned by Germans. Local newspapers described the attacks as the result of 'indignation at cold-blooded murder'. The news that the Germans had executed the British nurse, Edith Cavell, hit local newspapers on 18 October. The people of Manchester were more incensed than most as the martyred nurse, who was tending wounded soldiers in Belgium when sentenced to death, had worked for the Manchester and Salford Sick Poor and Private Nursing Institution in 1906 and the city had adopted her as one of its own.

The first protests were non violent: a factory in Trafford Park which employed Germans was forced to close when dockers threatened to blacklist it. The box manufacturer Messrs Hugh Stevenson, of Pollard Street, Ancoats, employed 600, mostly women and five men of German birth or ancestry. At 11 am on 11 May the women went on strike in protest against the employment of Germans. Resentment had been growing for some time. Though Mr Stevenson explained that the men had been at the factory for twenty years – one had a son in the Royal Marines and another was British-born – and were key workers as they alone could operate vital German machinery, the crowd outside the factory grew increasingly volatile. Some women became hysterical and the crowd was swelled by children waving Union Jacks. While the men were smuggled away in a canal boat, the workers agreed to return to work, though others remained outside.

But it wasn't long before things turned nasty. The Oldham Road – New Cross area of the city centre was known for its pork butchers, many of whom were German. A gang

Victoria Station, where many thousands of wounded soldiers arrived throughout the war.
Mark Flynn Postcards

of mill girls broke the windows and looted the produce of one such, a Mr Chris Samet, a naturalised British subject. Order was restored only with the intervention of a large body of police, including many special constables. Mr Samet was popular with locals, having lived in the area and had his shop there for twenty years and a number of soldiers on leave helped board up the shop and tidy up.

Yet one eye-witness felt no regrets: 'There wasn't much sympathy when their shops were looted and broken into. I didn't blame the people what did it because I knew their bitterness was there and I knew the Germans had really asked for it this time.'

There were also disturbances in other areas – High Town, Collyhurst, Oldham Road, Gorton, Ashton New Road, Abbey Hey Lane, Chancery Lane, Rusholme Road and Oxford Street. A German wholesale butcher in Ardwick had the windows of his living quarters smashed and his stock looted and in Garnett Street, High Town, a large contingent of police was required to drive looters from another German shop. The most extensive damage, however, was done to two butchers at the Bradford and Clayton end

of Ashton Old Road, who had their premises wrecked and stock looted. The police who attended were at first overwhelmed and it was only with the help of substantial reinforcements that they were able to restore order.

The response of the authorities was measured and firm. Thomas Fletcher and Thomas Bailey of Oldham Road were convicted of being drunk and disorderly while participating in the attack on a butcher's near their homes. Both men were fined 5/-. On 30 May thirty enemy alien shopkeepers were taken into custody at the Town Hall for their own safety.

The arrival of the first casualties of German poison gas on 10 May sparked renewed attacks, more serious than anything that preceded them. Thought the police enlisted the support of every available special constable and on occasion the assistance of soldiers, they found it impossible to quell the disturbances, which spread over a far wider area of working class Manchester than previously. The fire brigade was called out to Abbey Hey, where a crowd of thousands wrecked and torched a pork butcher's. In Clowes Street the house of an old lady believed to be German was fired after the crowd had first wrecked her home and destroyed all her furniture. Large numbers of police, including mounted officers, could do little to stop the destruction of a dozen shops in Collyhurst, Beswick, Ardwick, Oldham Road, Ashton Old Road, Rusholme, Bradford and Clayton. Pubs and restaurants were wrecked and three shops on Regent Road were destroyed as the police were outnumbered by an enormous mob. When officers took several men back to the police station an irate mob followed them, demanding their immediate release.

During the evening twenty Germans presented themselves at the Town Hall and police stations seeking protection. The Chief Constable, Mr Peacock, was so alarmed that he arrested all enemy aliens in areas where violence had broken out. These events coincided with reports of the Germans crucifying a captured Canadian near Ypres.

Anti-German sentiment led to another surge of army volunteers. After a decline towards the end of 1914, the number was again on the rise, with 370 putting themselves forward on 4 January alone and 1,000 the following week. Recruitment meetings were held every day in Piccadilly Gardens and daily soldiers marched through the city to the accompaniment of a band. This proved to be a powerful recruitment tool: when the Manchester battalions marched out on 7 December 1914 they attracted forty men who fell in, to the acclaim of the crowd, and marched off with them to be sworn in. By the end of January 1915, when over half those eligible had already joined up, volunteers were still presenting themselves at the rate of 1,000 a week.

Creator of Britain's New Armies, Lord Kitchener, taking the salute on the steps of Manchester Town Hall, March 1915. Taylor Library

On Sunday, 21 March Kitchener himself boosted the city's recruitment drive. In bright sunshine, especially welcome after the recent blizzards, he told a large crowd in Albert Square of the continuing need for recruits. Commending the men who paraded before him, he also praised the city for its 'exemplary patriotism.' As the men marched away singing

We don't like drill
It makes us ill,
But we do like a nice mince pie,

an old soldier standing near the dais remarked that in the thirty years he had known Kitchener it was the first time he had seen him smile.

The rapport between the crowd and men was remarkable – sisters, wives and sweethearts reached out to sons, husbands and fiancés. The *Manchester Guardian* captured the spirit of what it described as a thing of 'unqualified beauty'. 'We are living

history. Manchester's army is Manchester and the New Army is Britain, in a way no soldiers ever have been before. The people who cheered and the people who marched were not spectators and a spectacle: they were kin.'

The social pressure on men of military age became such that those who had not joined up because they worked in one of the city's 140 companies involved in war work wanted some proof that they were neither slackers nor cowards. On April 23 these men were issued with distinctive badges.

Yet by October 1915 volunteers had dwindled to a trickle: only sixty Mancunians put themselves forward on 18 October. As the realities of a seemingly endless conflict became apparent, enthusiasm for military service evaporated almost as quickly as it had arisen and many who had joined up regretted it. On 19 October the first case of its type appeared in the local court: Sydney and Florence Wallace, shopkeepers from Chancery Lane, Ardwick, were sentenced to seven days imprisonment for attempting to conceal Thomas Brown, a deserter.

In November Lord Derby announced that 'a measure of compulsion' for single men was on the way. This prompted many unmarried men to rush to the colours. The Manchester public felt conscription was long overdue. The announcement also led to a rush to munitions work, which it was generally believed would ensure exemption from military service. As the manager of one of Manchester's largest munitions factories put it, since Lord Derby began hinting that conscription was imminent, 'I have received a great number of applications for unskilled and semi-skilled jobs' and he knew that other firms involved in war work had experienced the same.

Those who rushed to the colours at the end of 1915 were often not the finest physical specimens. One recruiting station rejected fifty per cent of applicants as unfit. Yet a new record for volunteers was set on Wednesday, 9 December, as men queued four deep at the Town Hall from first thing in the morning throughout the day. From December, rejected men received an armlet to protect them from accusations of cowardice.

However, men of military age were by no means the only ones offering to serve. Early in the war communities throughout the city came together to form branches of the Red Cross. Their first decision was always the same: establish and equip their own hospital or support an existing one? Some of the new hospitals were in surprising locations.

Men of the Manchester Pals battalions marching through the streets of Manchester towards the Town Hall to be reviewed by Lord Kitchener, Sunday, 21 March 1915. Taylor Library

By 1915 Polefield Hall, Prestwich had been fitted out as a Red Cross hospital for twenty patients cared for by local volunteers under the guidance of a matron. Patients included Belgian citizens. As the number of military casualties grew, so the number of medical professionals available to treat civilians shrank. Later in the year this led to the closure of a number of hospital outpatients' departments throughout the city.

In March 1915 the War Authorities took over the new elementary school at Heald

Place as a hospital. Other schools earmarked for the purpose were at George Street, Alfred Street, Lily Lane and Moseley Road.

Soldiers convalescing in Lancashire Cricket Club looked out on the immaculate pitch and the famous club bar now functioned as a pharmacy, the only remnant of its former life an advert for *Johnnie Walker*. One local undertook to supply the staff and patients with all the bacon they could eat. In fact, the great flood of donations to hospitals and convalescent homes that characterized the early months of the war continued undiminished.

On 11 May the first victims of German gas attacks began to arrive at the Second Western General, Whitworth Street, bringing the total number of patients there to 8,000. Their progress through the city aroused both the sympathy and the outrage of those who cheered them. Many were clearly in an appalling condition, blinded and blistered, while others had suffered such damage to their lungs that they could barely draw breath.

As a child growing up in Levenshulme during the war, Joe Carley was fascinated and awed by the seemingly endless stream of military ambulances, each with its big red crosses, passing along Stockport Road en route to the military hospitals in the south of the city. Despite their familiarity, people never ignored them: an ambulance never passed without children waving.

Wounded soldiers were from the beginning of the war the focus of spontaneous demonstrations of affection and appreciation. Strangers frequently stopped them in the street and gave them cigarettes, fruit and chocolate and their arrival in the city and progress to hospital invariably evoked cheers from passers-by.

Nursing, one of the few types of work deemed suitable for a middle class girl, offered the opportunity to give direct succour to 'our gallant boys'. Former Suffragettes – largely middle class women of substance – were at the forefront of war service, filling the ranks of the VAD (Voluntary Defence Detachment), the Women's Emergency Corps, the Women's Defence Relief Corps and the Women's Hospital Corps. VADs had to be well-off because they were required to buy their own uniform, which at £22 was beyond the means of all but the comfortable middle-class. At its peak there were 3,575 VADs working in Manchester, many for whom charitable work was simply part of their social scene.

Women who joined the Women's Army Auxiliary Corps were also invariably from comfortable backgrounds. They were to be seen several evenings a week drilling in Chetham's yard. Members of the Women's National Land Service Corps, which became the Land Army in 1915, were, as one member recalls, 'girls from rather good homes'.

There were also hundreds of unobtrusive women who ensured that at whatever time of day or night a train carrying wounded soldiers arrived, someone was always there to provide refreshments. In total five million troops passed through Manchester and the YMCA raised £105,000 to ensure that not one of them went without a cup of tea and slice of toast. In addition, many elderly ladies, owners of the city's villa residences, posted signs at their gates: Wounded Soldiers May Rest in this Garden.

Manchester and Salford made up the largest military hospital centre in Britain. By the end of the war over 1,000 hospital trains carrying 180,000 wounded men had arrived in the city. Unsurprisingly, nurses seemed to be everywhere. With their grey bonnets tied in a bow under the chin, their long travelling cloaks – emblazoned between the shoulder blades with the pink Alexandra rose – and ankle-length dresses, the women of Queen Alexandra's Imperial Military Nursing Service were identical to their mothers who had nursed during the Boer War, still wearing the uniform designed by Florence Nightingale. Antiquated it may have been, but for ladies of a certain class, it was *de rigueur*. The Duchess of Sutherland, who was nursing in Belgium within days of the outbreak of war, was the role model for the daughters of the well-connected. As one of them put it, 'suddenly, the one autumn fashion everyone wanted to be seen wearing was a nurse's uniform'.

The number of civilians requiring hospital treatment suddenly rose from dusk on 1 March 1915 when the night-time city was plunged into darkness that did not lift until the end of the war. Lights were dimmed so that they could not be seen from above; illuminated shop fronts and advertising hoardings were banned. All windows in homes and places of work had to be curtained and the intensity of domestic lights was reduced. Lighting on trams, trains and cabs was reduced to such an extent that it was totally ineffective and with street lights daubed with 'pinky paint', which cast all residual light downwards, pedestrians risked their lives every time they attempted to cross a road after dark. Canals and rivers became death traps into which the unwary and inebriated fell with frightening regularity. The markets, once great pools of light and excitement lit up with flares and lamps, were plunged into darkness. The death toll began to rise immediately, reached its peak in November 1915 and the unusually high rates lasted right to the final days of the war.

The blackout was to prevent German aircraft finding Manchester, but everyone agreed: the effect was deeply depressing. Fewer people were on the streets at night and those who were faced a new danger, evident the first evening the regulations were in force when two trams collided on Oxford Street.

Rumours flourished in the darkened streets. Many believed that the threat of air raids was minimal. So what was the real reason for the blackout? Some said it was simply a 'cute dodge' to save money on street lighting, while a correspondent to a local newspaper was convinced that it was 'nothing but a kill-joy exercise', which would eventually lead to the 'closing of pubs at 10.30'. 'After that,' he opined, 'anyone caught smiling in public will be fined 5/- and the penalty for enjoying oneself will be instant death without the option of a chuckle.'

There was a general feeling that the authorities were covering up the number of accidents caused by the blackout. On 23 April 53-year-old Charles Lane became the third Whitefield fatality in a week, when he was crushed under the wheels of his own vehicle. On 29 April a prominent Burnley manufacturer, Mr Jesse Simpson, lost his life in road traffic accident in Whalley Range. On 2 November two people – a boy of 14 and a woman of 69 – were killed by motor vehicles. With the death of 11-year-old Leonard Jones, crushed under a car on Forge Lane in East Manchester, on 5 November, the coroner Mr C.C.W. Surridge, said 'something would have to be done' and expressed the views of most Mancunians when he said, 'precautions can be carried to a ridiculous extent'.

Contrary to all expectations, even after 10-year-old Annie Dorrington was killed as

Taylor Bros, one of the city's major producers of war material. Mark Flynn Postcards

she crossed Stockport Road on her way to church, the Chief Constable announced new, more rigorous, lighting restrictions. Now motor vehicles were not allowed to show headlights and sidelights had to be screened while street lighting was further dimmed.

Yet there was at least one way in which things were improving. Towards the end of 1914 the government began to appreciate the war could not be won without the rapid expansion of engineering work. Over 10,000 engineers had joined up in the early months of the war and it was essential that women fill the gaps. In fact, the demand for labour was such that the Manchester tramp ward at the Workhouse, the largest in England, was almost empty and Strangeways Prison was only half full.

Already the war had transformed the fortunes of many Manchester companies, none more so than Avro, the aircraft manufacturer. At the start of the war it was barely surviving but the change to mass production enabled the Avro 540 to become an effective front line aircraft and the training plane of the Royal Flying Corps. Soon the company moved to bigger premises at Newton Heath and developed plants at Heaton Chapel and Gorton. Women formed a crucial part of its wartime workforce, earning between 12/- and 15/- for a fifty-three-hour week. This was where the big money was in war work - - not in munitions but in engineering, where women on piece work were commonly earning between £2 and £3 a week.

The importance of munitions production was brought home to the city on 3 June when Lloyd George, Minister for Munitions, met trade union leaders in the Midland

Workers in a Gorton munitions factory.
Mark Flynn Postcards

Hotel. The result was the establishment of the Manchester Munitions Committee designed to increase production. The great man also spoke to the workers and, according to one, 'brought home to us that guns and shells are the things that really matter'. The head of a large West Gorton arms manufacturer struck a less harmonious note expressing his hope that the minister's visit would mean 'no more slacking and no more disputes'.

The terms of the 1914 Defence of the Realm Act (DORA) relating to labour were designed to prevent precisely these problems and employers used them to the full. On 29 June six youths appeared before the City Police Court, charged with being absent from work in a munitions factories in Higher Openshaw and Bradford for one half-day. Each was ordered to pay 30/- to his employer but was told that if he behaved himself in future this might not be enforced. Another worker, Patrick Connell, was fined in his absence the enormous sum of £10 for a similar offence.

The Munitions War Act also provided means to encourage slackers. The first prosecutions under the Act were held at the Town Hall on Friday 30 July when thirty-two men employed by Craven Bros Ltd, Reddish, were brought before the Recorder charged with going on strike over wages and working conditions without first submitting the matter to the Board of Trade. The men pleaded ignorance of the law and Mr A.J. Ashton took a lenient view, fining each man 2/6 with 42/- costs.

Munitions workers were the new aristocracy of labour, reputedly earning obscene wages, which allowed them to consume enormous qualities of beer. Some argued there was little else for them to do as there were so few alternative sources of entertainment available. When war broke out and Manchester City's practice match at Hyde Road, scheduled for that weekend, went ahead as planned, as did the race meeting at Manchester Race Course, it seemed normal social life would be unaffected by the conflict. Mr Wu continued to wow audiences at the Princes and the other music halls reported no shortage of customers. It was not long, however, before letters demanding the suspension of all frivolous distractions, out of respect for those dying at the front, became a staple of local newspapers.

This attitude was to gain increasing support among the Manchester elite as the war progressed, though working men became impatient of what they regarded as a puritanical begrudging of the distractions which lifted the gloom of war. Amateur sports clubs of all sorts, for instance, were closing down as their members flocked to the colours; and by the end of 1914 many were defunct. Yet the professionals continued as usual. Thirty thousand fans packed into Hyde Road to watch Manchester United hang on for an undeserved draw against Manchester City, whose attacks were spearheaded by the speedy Billy Meredith, the most esteemed player in the history of the city. Despite predictions to the contrary, theatres and music halls were relatively little affected while picture houses suffered not at all. The steeplechase meeting at Castle Irwell in March 1915 drew an enormous crowd of 7,000 spectators. Manchester City's matches at Hyde Road continued to attract big crowds, among the most loyal supporters being the engineers working for Armstrong-Whitworth's, Beyer-Peacock and other companies in the east of the city, near the ground and mostly engaged in war work.

On 24 April it was announced that Old Trafford was to host the FA Cup Final between Sheffield United and Chelsea, much to the annoyance of Mr F.N. Charrington, who

The Hippodrome, one of the city's largest music halls, which continued to attract big crowds during the war. Mark Flynn Postcards

promptly convened a meeting at Albert Hall, Peter Street, to protest against the match 'during the present crisis'. The local press was unsympathetic to the philanthropist's cause, and believed the match would 'provide recreation for many thousands of people who need and deserve it'. Mancunians' attitudes varied, but the man who was 'filled with contempt for the short-sighted interfering persons of the kill-joy type who are doubtless at the back of this agitation' seems representative of opinion. Lord Derby himself presented the cup to the victorious Blades.

It was not only over sport that tempers flared. The staples of working class life – food, shelter, work and drink all occasioned violent disagreement.

In January 1915 one local newspaper estimated that the increase in food prices had reduced the real income of working class families by as much as twenty-five per cent and to such an extent that such luxuries as 'tinned fruit, canned fish and jam were no longer making even an occasional appearance in the household'. A local reporter visited a grocer's in one of the poorer parts of the city and compared current with pre-war prices: the increase was twenty-eight per cent. What made matters worse was that fish, once a cheap substitute for meat, was now prohibitively expensive. An average working class family ate three to four loaves of bread daily – more when other foods were in short supply. By the end of May the price of a loaf of bread in Manchester had risen by seventy-five per cent since the outbreak of war.

In addition, the price of coal and coke was abnormally high. By April the price of coke had reached 1/- a hundredweight, twice the pre-war price. There were power cuts as supplies of both gas and electricity were periodically shut off. In May, gas went up by twenty per cent per thousand cubic feet. The coal shortage was exacerbated in July 1915 when for a short time all the Welsh pits were idle due to a miners' strike.

Accommodation, another basic need, was also rising in price. When war began there was already a housing famine in Manchester and the problem of rising rents, which was to become a major working class grievance in the city, was already a cause of contention by September 1914. A number of landlords appealed to the courts for assistance in evicting tenants who were in rent arrears. The City Stipendiary Magistrate, Mr Edgar Brierley, made it clear that no eviction order could be enforced without a summons, in regard to which the tenant had a right to appear and explain why it should not be enforced. This was a clear reference to the plight of those families which faced eviction because the bread-winner had joined up.

Landlords claimed that with rising local taxes and the increased cost of repairs and maintenance they had little choice but to increase rents. But tenants were determined to resist and in August 1915 the newly formed Tenants' Association told its members in Cheetham, Openshaw, Gorton, Hulme, Moss Side, Chorlton-on-Medlock, Chorlton-cum-Hardy and Levenshulme not to pay increased rents but to declare a rent strike. The Association claimed that increases were far beyond anything that could be justified by increased costs. One landlord had increased rents three times since the outbreak of war, which was particularly onerous for clerks and shop assistants, whose salaries had not risen.

The issue raised its head in an emotive manner in October 1915 when a woman who had received notice of a rent increase forwarded the letter to her husband in France. His response, published in a local paper, embarrassed unscrupulous landlords. The corporal suggested the landlord should join him in France for his second winter campaign and see some of the sights of desolation he was enduring. 'You might not then,' the soldier added, 'be so eager to raise the rent of a man who is doing his bit to keep you and the likes of you in comfort at home.' The corporal's wife explained that her assured income amounted to 13/- a week, of which the increased rent would account for half. Before the war her husband had earned £2 a week. Unlike many other men, he did not receive any pay from his employer while serving.

On 23 November the government finally took action. Introducing the Rent and Mortgage Interest (War Restrictions) Bill, Mr Long acknowledged that 'rent-raising had produced a very deep feeling of bitterness and resentment that was a danger to society'.

With sharp rises in outgoings it is little wonder that workers demanded improved wages. Industrial disputes became a part of everyday life. The first was in January 1915, when Mr R. Blundell, Secretary of the Dockers' Union, demanded an additional shilling a day for his members at the Port of Manchester, citing the increase in food prices as justification. The dockers settled for one penny on their hourly rate. In September they demanded another rise and during the course of the year Manchester workers on the railways and the United Carters' Association gained increases.

Manchester engineers felt that the rising prices which were enriching the wealthy were squeezing their miserable living standards. In March, local engineers demanded 5/- a week rise but settled for 3/-. But the engineers' grievances were not simply about pay. As skilled craftsmen they were jealous of their status and anxious to ensure that women did not encroach on their work. They were also unhappy at having to work excessively long hours, many getting off only one Sunday a month. The extent of this problem is illustrated by the case of Messrs Humphries, Jackson & Abler Ltd, metal workers, of Hawkins Street, Old Trafford who were brought before the Manchester Police Court charged with two instances of employing boys after the proper time at night and one of employing them on Sundays. One boy, Arthur Mosford, worked a seventy-five hour week, including an eighteen hour shift, while another, William Johnson, did sixty-six hours a week and one shift of sixteen hours. The company was fined and warned.

After working such long hours, men liked nothing better than a pint. It's hard to exaggerate the importance of pubs in the life of the city's working people. Every street had at least one. One-sixth of working class income was spent on drink and Manchester had a well-deserved reputation for its riotous drinking culture.

From the first days of the war there was agitation for restrictions on the availability of alcohol, which quickly gathered momentum among non-conformist and evangelical groups, who alleged an increase in excessive drinking, especially among women. The Temperance Society wanted nothing less than total abstinence for the duration, citing the saving of food this would achieve. *The Manchester Evening News* was not convinced, dismissing their claims as 'greatly exaggerated'.

The first inkling of restrictions on drinking was broached in March when the Chairman of the Licensing Committee expressed his dismay at seeing so many soldiers and workmen drunk first thing in the morning. He was, he said, personally in favour of restricting licensing hours. Before the war pubs could in effect open when they chose and most did so for eighteen hours a day. In areas where many workmen were out and about early in the morning, pubs were open to provide food as well as alcoholic drink.

The fears of the licensees were justified: the military authorities decreed that from Monday, 29 March pubs could open only from 10.30 am to 10 pm and on Sundays from 12.30 pm to 2.30 pm and then from 6.30 pm to 9.30 pm. Publicans immediately complained that these restrictions were bound to lead to redundancies among bar staff. Many others announced their intention to leave the trade, citing the decline in custom since the outbreak of the war.

Meanwhile the local papers were reminding Mancunians that Lord Kitchener, following the splendid example of His Majesty King George V, had foresworn drink for the duration. Throughout Manchester and Salford more and more men were carrying discrete pledge cards in red, white and blue, proclaiming their commitment to the Follow the King movement. Other notable abstainers were Lloyd George, Arthur Conan Doyle, John Galsworthy and the poet laureate, Robert Bridges. Nevertheless, a motion by Councillor H. Wood that Manchester City Council follow their example was carried only at the second attempt and then only after heated exchanges.

In May 1915 at the annual meeting of W. G. Armstrong Whitworth & Co Ltd, Openshaw – the largest engineers in the area, and now entirely devoted to arms production – Mr J.M. Falkiner, vice-chairman, complained of the loss of production due

Wife of the Manchester Brigade's commander, Mrs Westropp, presenting prizes at the Brigade's first sports day, 21 April 1915. Taylor Library

to 'a minority whose irregular habits lowered the general level of output', an oblique reference to heavy drinking among armaments workers. On the other hand, the Shudehill licensees were telling anyone who would listen that the new licensing restrictions had them staring at 'utter ruin'. These pubs depended very largely on early morning trade, chiefly from workers at Smithfield Market and market gardeners who left home at midnight, dropped their goods at Smithfield and then took refreshment before returning home.

The takings of suburban pubs were unaffected: patrons simply drank the same amount in less time and bought more to drink at home. But overall brewers were suffering and one of the largest, with its head office in Manchester, reported a fall of forty per cent in profits. Many pubs were panic buying spirits, convinced that the government would soon ban them.

In May 1915 much to the chagrin of drinkers, new minimum beer taxes were introduced throughout the city. Draught beer was now 3d a pint. Yet as the war wore on concerns about excessive drinking among women, often assumed to be well-paid munitions workers, continued to grow and found frequent expression in local newspapers.

Heaton Park Sports Day, 21 April 1915. Around 20,000 spectators gathered to witness the event. Present were The Lord Mayor, Lord Derby, the Chief Constable and General Westropp. Taylor Library

Even the most intoxicated could not fail to notice how their city had changed by the end of the first complete year of conflict: Manchester was totally given over to war. It felt the impact of the conflict uniquely: not only was the drain on its manpower more acute than in any other city – by December 1915, 100,000 Mancunians had joined up – but it was within easy reach of the great army training grounds, was home to one of the largest military hospitals in the kingdom, was an important centre of munitions production and had through the enormous array of charitable and other voluntary organizations demonstrated a keen interest in the welfare of its troops, their dependants and our Allies. Seventeen months of war had transformed the city.

And bigger changes were about to occur.

Chapter Three

1916: High Hopes and Hostility

'We never owned a conscious. But we know what is right.'

THE CITY WAS agog with rumours: any day now there would be an enormous Allied attack in the west, which would drive back the Germans and bring the war to a speedy end. After the disaster of Gallipoli in 1915, when hundreds of Manchester men lost their lives in a campaign that ended in an ignominious withdrawal, the city was desperate for some good news. As 1916 unfolded and one mishap was heaped upon another – the Easter Rising in Ireland, the losses at Jutland and Kitchener's death – people invested more and more hope in the 'big push', which was to break German resistance and secure victory.

In January 1916 the 1st, 2nd, 3rd and 4th Manchester Pals took up their positions north of the Somme. During February, the 5, 6 and 7 Battalions joined them. From May, local newspapers were full of reports of enormous German losses at Verdun and accounts of starving German soldiers, the Kaiser going mad and the imminent collapse of the enemy front. In the city it seemed certain that the next big attack, expected at any moment, would bring victory.

Heaton Park Camp: Men of the First Brigade, Manchester Regiment, at training. Taylor Library

Heaton Park Camp: Officers at revolver practice on one of the purpose built ranges.
Taylor Library

Yet it is hard to be optimistic when you are hungry and hunger was a common condition for many Mancunians. A survey of suburban grocers showed that since the outbreak of war the price of bacon had increased by seventy-two per cent, butter by sixty-six per cent, cheese by fifty per cent, sugar by 450 per cent and jam by 380 per cent – always with the proviso that they could be obtained. Prices also fluctuated from day-to-day, though the trend was relentlessly upwards. Board of Trade figures showed that food prices generally had increased by seventy-eight per cent since the war began.

By the end of the year it was clear that there was a thriving black market operating even in basic foodstuff: in October several bakers in Greenheys were prosecuted for selling bread 'other than by weight'. The shortage of flour became more and more acute as the year progressed. In November the weight of standard loaves was reduced by one ounce.

By March the shortage of sugar was so acute that there were many houses in the city without any and many grocers had none to sell. It is important to remember that doctors at this time believed that sugar was essential to children's healthy development. Cafés, too, were getting less than half the sugar they needed. The situation was made worse in April when the government imposed a tax on sugar, together with cocoa, coffee, soft drinks and bicycles, railway travel and, worst of all, all forms of entertainment. In some cases the latter doubled the cost of going to the picture palace.

People blamed producers and grocers for holding back supplies and otherwise exploiting the situation and a series of prominent court cases seemed to confirm this view. On 22 June a number of milk dealers appeared before the city magistrates accused of adulterating their wares. One, James Makin of Upper Medlock Street, Hume, had added, in what was his second offence, sixteen per cent water to his milk. He was fined £10 and ordered to pay the expenses of witnesses.

Milk was again in the news in September, when many of the city's dealers complained that farmers in the Cheshire Milk Producers' Association were demanding the exorbitant price of 4½d a quart. The dealers resolved not to pay it. By October this dispute led to a shortage of milk in the city and a significant fall in consumption. By the end of the month reports began to appear claiming that the poor, for whom milk formed a significant part of their diet, were suffering terribly. One Shudehill dealer claimed that both farmers and milk merchants were holding back supplies in order to inflate prices. 'The government,' he said, 'should take action in the interests of the people.'

This, of course, fuelled the debate about rising food prices, especially of cheese, bacon and butter. Cheese was a staple of poor households, with the result that its ever rising price had a disproportionate effect on the worst off. All of these products were affected by supply problems. The Manchester and Salford War Problems Committee was so concerned that on 4 November it convened a meeting of all Lancashire and Cheshire MPs to discuss the issue. Its purpose was simply to put pressure on the government to 'deal effectively with the increasing cost of food.'

The public were not alone in suffering from rising food prices. By 1916 it was evident that many shopkeepers were forced to close their doors for good as empty shops became a feature of virtually every street. Butchers suffered especially. Those who managed to stay in business suffered another blow on 21 October when the government announced that all shops must close Monday to Friday at 7 pm. Suburban shopkeepers in particular protested that this would put them out of business as they were largely dependent on customers buying after work. The authorities clearly accepted that they had a case, for at the end of the month they relented and allowed them an additional hour during the week and until 9 pm on a Saturday. Yet the public remained convinced that the food trade, at all levels, was exploiting them.

By November many stall holders in Smithfield claimed that potatoes had become a luxury. Selling at the unprecedented price of 2d a pound, many customers could afford no more than a single pound. Fruit and vegetables were selling at between twice and three times pre-war prices. The street hawkers had virtually disappeared from the city. In December the City Council appointed a committee to formulate a plan for growing potatoes in the city.

To promote the scheme the Parks Department announced on 17 March a training course for women gardeners at Heaton Park, designed to help them into employment in agriculture. The Department also staged 'how to economise' demonstrations for the housewife at Milton Hall, Deansgate, including one showing how to cook a complete dinner for five people at no more than 4d a head. Miss Petty, the 'Pudding Lady,' demonstrated how to make cakes and puddings without eggs, while a dressmaker demonstrated how to make garments from rags and amazed her audience by producing a boy's suit from an old cloak which she assured everyone 'the ragman refused to give 2d for'.

The National War Savings Committee wanted people to eat less meat. This request raised the hackles of many Mancunians, who complained that not only was meat beyond the means of the city's poor, but so were the alternatives. Regardless, the Committee asked everyone to have one meatless day a week – a clear demonstration of the extent to which the government was out of touch with the lives of ordinary people.

Local agencies, however, were fully aware of the extent of problems. Opening the November meeting of the Manchester War Problems Committee, Councillor R.J. Davies spoke of the 'seething discontent of the working classes of Manchester with regard to food prices'. The problem of the poor was compounded as they were forced to buy both food and coal in the most uneconomical way – in small quantities. Davies stoked the fires of resentment against suppliers by claiming that 'there was more profit made of food than munitions and other essentials for the continuance of the war'.

When the government finally took decisive action by appointing a Food Controller in November the immediate effect was a sharp rise in the price of white flour as a result of panic buying in middle class parts of the city. Lord Devonport's first act was to decree that white flour was no longer to be milled. He pegged milk prices, reduced sweet manufacturing and brought the sale and distribution of food under his control. The situation was so serious that the Lord Mayor, Alderman Smedhurst, convened a meeting at the Town Hall to discuss the whole food issue and specifically the milk situation. Many people were finding that grocers sold commodities in short supply, such as sugar, only to customers who spent a substantial amount. There was a great deal of discontent about hotels and restaurants having seemingly limitless amounts of food, too much of which, it was claimed, was wasted. Mrs Annot Robinson of the Women's War Interests Committee weighed in claiming that those suffering most in Manchester were women living on a small army allowance. 'Many of these poor people,' she said, 'are reduced to living on tea, bread and margarine. Their hardship is becoming intolerable.' A mother of five children told her she could afford only one bottle of milk a week.

Shopkeepers were also at pains to stress their problems. Mr T. Burrows, chairman of the Manchester Retail Traders' Association, complained bitterly about the disastrous effects of the new lighting restrictions. 'Shops and streets,' he said, 'are thrown into absolute gloom to no purpose and traders are faced with a great deal of expense and trouble.'

By February over 200 people, mostly retailers, had been summoned for breaching lighting regulations. One shopkeeper, who insisted on burning a light which illuminated a large section of Market Street, had to pay a £2 fine. Many pleaded ignorance of the regulations and complained that they had received no prior warning. The rigour of the authorities in enforcing these regulations was no doubt the result of further Zeppelin raids in the south and east of the country. The raid of 1 February killed fifty-four and injured sixty-seven over six counties.

Partly to assuage the complaints of all those who felt that the blackout was imposing unnecessary hardship and danger on the population, the government introduced a daylight saving law, the Summer Time Act, which came into effect at 2 am on the night of 20 / 21 May, when all clocks were put forward to 3 am. Yet this did nothing to improve the situation during the hours of darkness, especially when the Gas Committee prohibited lighting in side streets. It is clear that there was a real fear of air raids among both the Manchester public and those in authority. The chief response to the blackout was that by 1916 many householders had painted their steps, gateposts and kerbs near their homes white. The Corporation had long since painted a white band around lampposts.

The dangers of the blackout were not only physical. On 25 October Councillor Kendall complained that it was having a baleful effect on the city's morals: he said the city's streets were 'no longer fit for respectable people to pass along' though several other councillors strongly contested this. All, however, agreed that 'the danger from the darkened streets was far greater than anything to be feared from the Zeppelins'.

The dark streets were only one of the many things changing the lives of children. In fact, there is a powerful argument for saying that Manchester more than any other city was transformed by the war. The immediate effect on schools, for instance, was that they went half-time and children attended either in the morning or the afternoon and were generally free to roam the streets for the rest of the day.

The role of teachers also changed: they served school meals, organized the children to bring in goods for sales of work to raise money for the troops, operated a school saving bank and later administered food rationing. They organized the children to make comforts – scarves, gloves, socks, and balaclavas – for the troops and taught them how to grow vegetables to overcome food shortage. Wool was delivered to schools for the children to knit body belts, socks and mittens for the troops.

When not in school, children suffered from the absence of their fathers. The serious

Kendall & Gent's, one of Manchester engineering works, which employed many women.
Mark Flynn Postcards

rise in juvenile crime at the beginning of the year continued. When the Recorder, Mr A.J. Ashton, opened the summer Assizes, he commented on the fact that seventeen of the prisoners before him were under 21 and eight under 18. All were charged with theft of various kinds and all sentenced to periods of Borstal training.

By November the authorities were in a panic about the spirit of lawlessness and rebellion among young people in what one magistrate described as 'the more poorly circumstanced walks of life'. The cause was clear to all: the absence of paternal control now that so many men were away at the front. Mothers, often working long hours in war industries, were unequal to the task of disciplining boisterous boys. Indiscipline was particularly affecting schools – where male teachers were now a rarity – to such an extent that the National Association of Teachers called on the War Office to ensure that at least some male teachers were not called up.

In many cases children whose fathers were at the front were also lacking maternal control as more and more women were drawn into work. The war, according to one commentator, 'transformed the city into one vast machine shop and war production factory'. The women in the munitions factories included former actresses, waitresses, typists, dressmakers and those who had never previously worked. Since August 1914 the output of Manchester workshops had tripled and more than half the population of Manchester was involved in turning out war materials.

However, there was mounting discontent among the city's 10,000 women working in the munitions industry. One factory alone employed 2,000 women. Mrs A. Robinson, a champion of women's causes and Mrs J.E. Tomlinson, chairman of the Manchester and Salford District Women's War Interests Committee, both protested that women were in many cases doing the same work as men for much less pay. Few Manchester factories, they claimed, followed government recommendations of a flat rate for women of at least £1 a week. Some firms, they claimed, 'are making women slave for their patriotism'. These women, like all munitions workers, could leave bad employers only with a release certificate, which the bosses often refused to issue. One woman told the Committee that for working night shifts she was being paid only 13/3 a week, less than a third of the male wage.

By 1916 it was commonplace to find women doing jobs formerly the preserve of men. They were now an accepted sight on railway platforms, as clerks in post offices, banks and commercial establishments, as post women and van drivers. By February 1916 there were 250 women working on the Manchester trams and one manager reported that 'tramway passengers are evidently well pleased as they get nothing but praise from the public'. One bank manager employing many women went so far as to say, 'In some respects they are better than men – more industrious and more careful'. What's more, he opined, they undoubtedly had a civilizing and humanizing effect on the crusty old fogies to be found among the staff of any bank. He was confident that 'they have come to stay'. By March 1916 the shortage of men forced the Watch Committee to consider the request of the National Union of Women Workers and the Manchester and Salford Women Citizens' Association that more women be employed by the police.

Like their male counterparts, women in virtually every industry were finding their wages lagging far behind rising prices. According to reports in local newspapers, married soldiers were unhappy that their wives working in industry were being underpaid. Even when cotton spinners – largely women – reluctantly settled for their second five per cent rise within a year, Mr Mullins, union secretary, complained that rising prices meant that his workers were in real terms worse off than at the start of the year.

Most workers agreed. In June the dockers renewed their claim for a one penny an hour increase. Their dispute spread to Runcorn and all those working on the Bridgewater Canal. By mid July the dockers were threatening to strike, a threat which 4,000 of them carried out on 14 July, bringing the entire docks to a standstill. Their union officials urged them to remain at work but they refused, claiming that the employers' delaying tactics were insulting and their offer of a halfpenny an hour increase derisory; they would settle for nothing less than the full penny. Three days later they agreed to resume work on the understanding that Mr P.W. Atkins, the Salford Stipendiary Magistrate, would immediately begin an arbitration process.

On 11 September engineers demanded an additional 9/- a week. One factor inflaming the ire of these key workers was the employers' use of the police, who could be seen every day in the streets around engineering works arresting absentees – in a single weekend they arrested sixty-seven men who subsequently appeared in court. Others were arrested for failing to register under the National Registration Act, 1915. This Act required everyone between the ages of 15 and 65 who was not in the Armed Forces to register with the government. It was generally seen as a step towards compulsory military service. It was clear that industrial harmony was under a great deal of strain.

In September the railway workers demanded a 10/- a week rise. Almost immediately their demand was met in full, but only because the government agreed to fund part of the cost. In November the Government Production Committee awarded the engineers and allied trades a 3/- a week rise.

Strikes and the threat of strikes added to the hostility with which munitions workers were regarded. More than one diarist described them as 'the lowest form of life'. Tales of their exorbitant wages and the frequency with which they downed tool made them unpopular and they were frequently abused in the streets. Yet demands on their wages and on all those in employment were increasing daily. The government continually reminded the public that the cost of the war was immense – £5,710,000 a day by 1918. To meet this staggering expense, everyone was encouraged to save their excess cash, no matter how little, in war bonds. Every school had a 'penny bank' in which children deposited their coppers until they accumulated the 15s 6d required to buy a Saving Certificate. Members of each of the local savings committees went around the local cinemas and music halls and spoke about the duty to save and thereby ensure a speedy end to the war. By October 1916 there were eighty-eight associations linked to the Manchester War Savings Central Committee. Civilians were constantly reminded that they should match the sacrifices of the men at the front.

In addition to the government's demands, there were also those of a bewildering array of war-related charities. A single charity, the Manchester and Salford district of the King's Lancashire Military Convalescent Hospital Fund sold 500,000 miniature flags in two days in September 1916. The people of Manchester could see how much the money was needed: Heaton Park alone was home to 4,000 convalescent soldiers.

TREAT FOR WOUNDED SOLDIERS.

In celebration of the French Flag Day eight hundred wounded soldiers, Red Cross Nurses, and soldiers' wives were entertained by Mr. Harry Leslie at the Rusholme Pavilion yesterday afternoon, an excellent performance being given by his company, the "Nobodies."

The Lord Mayor was among those present, and after addressing the audience from the stage he proposed a vote of thanks to the entertainers.

One of the many provisions made for entertaining wounded soldiers.

On 20 October it was impossible to walk down any of the city centre's streets without being confronted by one of the many hundreds of Red Cross fund-raisers, each carrying some of the two million flags produced for sale in the area. In additional to all the local fund-raising events, in June alone there were thirty-three national flag days. Yet the generosity of the public appeared inexhaustible.

There was, however, a general feeling that there were some who were abusing the generosity of others by refusing to do their bit. By the end of 1915 it was clear that volunteers were not presenting themselves in sufficient numbers to replace those killed and wounded at the front.

Early in the year it was reported that a million single men were still 'holding aloof'. Government press releases were clearly preparing the way for conscription, though there were still elements of the Liberal Party, socialists, trade unionists and those who objected on moral grounds, opposed to conscription. At the end of January 1916 there were 21,583 single and 25,942 married men in the city eligible for military service, few of whom showed any enthusiasm for military life.

Conscription came into effect in January 1916, when the Military Service Act empowered the government to compel men to serve in the armed forces. It was not implemented until June, by when there were tribunals to hear appeals for exemption. There was also a list of 'starred' occupations, workers in which would be exempt from military service because they were engaged in vital war work. In the weeks before June there was a renewed surge in volunteers, widely attributed to the desire of men who were sure to be conscripted to avoid the stigma of having 'been fetched' and hoping to enjoy a degree of choice in where they served, which would not be available to conscripts.

Despite hopes to the contrary, conscription proved to be a major cause of strife. Among the first to feel aggrieved were the many men who had previously volunteered and been rejected on medical grounds. They were dismayed to find themselves required to undergo a further medical examination. What is more, the government announced on 1 June that 'the vast majority of these men will be found fit for some sort of work or occupation in the army'. Those deemed unfit for service even by this new, less exacting standard, now demanded that they be issued with an armlet to verify their status and protect them from charges of cowardice. One such man complained bitterly to his local newspaper that having tried to enlist on five separate occasions, on each of which he was rejected on medical grounds, he still faced the prospect of being taken for a slacker. Men discharged from the service because of wounds were issued with a silver badge.

It is clear that the normal response to conscription in Manchester was to launch an appeal requesting exemption. Hearings took place after medical examination had been completed so that they excluded the unfit. About a quarter of all those who appealed were granted an exemption, usually temporary. Few people had any sympathy for those seeking 'special treatment' and the tribunals were inundated with anonymous letters denouncing 'shirkers'.

By early March the number of appeals was such that the Manchester tribunal had to split into four sections. A music hall act wanted a deferment to enable him to fulfil two contracts worth £15. A theology student at the Baptist College appealed on the grounds that priests of other Christian denominations were exempted. Both men were refused and the tribunals clearly agreed with the public perception that many young men, having failed to worm their way into starred occupations, were appealing for exemption on frivolous grounds. This view was certainly confirmed by a man who claimed he was vital to a variety dancing act, a single man who claimed that his role as a milkman meant he 'assisted in the bringing up of the children of the nation', a supporter of an aged mother and a restaurateur who appeared on behalf of a waiter on the grounds that he 'would rather have one man than three women'. Those in the food trade clearly had an aversion to army life, as another session of the tribunal involved the owner of a vegetarian restaurant appealing on behalf of an employee whose work 'involved feats of strength and intelligence'. His claim was disallowed too.

Those who were resolute and reasonably articulate, if not logical, were generally excused combat service. The Bishop of Manchester, Dr Knox, was unimpressed by many who appealed on religious grounds, commenting that he 'had never heard of God's name so often taken in vain as during tribunals'. The general public shared his contempt for those they regarded as trying evade their duty. In April one local newspaper accurately reflected the public mood in a series that ran for several days. 'The Conscientious Objector: What the Married Soldier Thinks of Him' began with a letter from a serving private who wrote, 'I call it nothing but cowardice which makes these men show the white feather'. In October another local paper ran a series of articles by 'A Manchester Lad' serving at the front. Speaking of 'conscies' he said, 'nine out of ten of them are hypocrites. It is not fair to us out here, especially those like me who have been fighting since 1914. There are thousands like me today. We never owned a conscience. But we know what is right.'

Also fiercely resented were the single men who refused to join up. Looking back almost seventy years later, Fred Roberts remembered vividly that as he marched through Manchester he 'felt bitter that morning, seeing all those young fellows going off to work to the offices and here was I, in the army, a married man of 31-years old.'

Meanwhile the appeal tribunals continued their work. One woollen salesman applied for exemption because he was planning marriage and had little chance of saving money in the army. Others appealed on the grounds that they were essential to the operation of the trade in which they were employed. The tribunal's military representative expressed his amazement that the city's working population consisted entirely of 'indispensable experts'. He had no more sympathy for the insurance clerk who sought exemption on the grounds that 'my mother would be unhappy if I went' or the man whose digestive system was so sensitive that he 'ate only bread and Lenten tea'. Unsurprisingly, all these appeals were rejected.

Some went further than pleading personal exemption: they sought to mobilize opinion against the principle of compulsion. The Salford and Manchester Anti-Conscription League held a conference in Manchester. Most of those who attended were men of army age, though there were also many women. The local police responded a few days later when on 23 June they raided the office of the No-Conscription Fellowship on Oxford Road, Fallowfield, confiscated all their records and arrested five men. The next day the defendants – a journalist, a furniture shop assistant, a newspaper clerk, a printer and an insurance clerk – were charged with being absent from the Army. One of the five, Harold Ernest Wild of Slade Grove, Longsight, claimed that he was entitled to exemption as a conscientious objector but had been wrongly directed to non-combatant service, which he refused. He claimed the tribunal had acted illegally in his case. The magistrate, Mr Armitage, was unimpressed and fined him £2, before directing that all five be handed over to the military authorities.

June 22 was a bad day for all those who thought like Wild, as the second Military Service Act came into effect making all men between 18 and 41 'now soldiers by law'. Even the world famous could not escape its reach, as John Donaldson, 'the Australian Blue Streak', discovered on 18 September. The world champion at his distance was arrested that morning in Wright Street, Greenheys and subsequently handed over to the military authorities as absent from His Majesty's Forces. Donaldson argued that as an Australian he was not subject to conscription in Britain. The Stipendiary, Mr Brierley, however, took the view that as someone normally resident in the country he was.

The rounding up of reluctant soldiers continued apace as police targeted lodging houses and arrested fifty absentees on 13 September alone. Before the court they offered a variety of explanations for their non-appearance. One, with touching modesty, said he hadn't turned up because he could not imagine the army wanting him, while another said 'he did not care much for army life'. Others, like Albert Shaw of Kay Street, Ardwick, had clearly given more thought to the matter: he had equipped himself with a bogus certificate of unfitness, which he had apparently stolen from a fellow lodger. He was sentenced to three months hard labour, after which he was to join his fellow defendants in the army.

Few, however, went as far as Robert Taylor in trying to avoid the military life. On 14 September he appeared in court charged with trying to shoot Inspector William Moore and evading arrest while being pursued as a deserter.

There were, at the other extreme, those who exploited the kudos of military service without any right to do so. Robert Edward Hall was one such. He wore three stripes on his shoulder – each indicating a war wound – and the ribbons of the VC and DCM and used the front of a war hero to defraud his Longsight landlady. In fact, Hall had been discharged from the army after thirty days' service as not likely to make an efficient soldier. The magistrate jailed him for six months.

Some found the prospect of the army intolerable. The unfortunate James Oswald of 253 Stockport Road shot himself in Victoria Park two days after receiving notice to return to his regiment. He was 26 years old and had just been discharged from the Whitworth Street Hospital complaining of 'pains in his head'.

In addition to conscription, new licensing restriction also came into effect in Manchester in January. 'Treating' and 'buying rounds' were banned as they were seen as one of the major causes of excessive drinking. What is more, the authorities actually enforced this regulation, as Agnes Graham, licensee of the Old House at Home, Hulme, and her customer, Rebecca Moore, discovered in May, when they appeared before the magistrate. Agnes had served Rebecca, knowing that she was buying drink for three friends and a soldier who happened to be standing at the bar. What neither knew was that the soldier was in fact Special Constable Balmer in disguise. The landlady was fined £2 and the customers 2/6 each.

On 28 August another raft of licensees and compulsively hospitable patrons appeared before the magistrate. William Henry Walker, licensee of the Submarine Bar, Spring Gardens, stood accused of the more serious offence of serving customers after hours. He was fined £3.

It became clear at the licensing meeting for the city on 2 February that the police were intent on closing pubs which sought to evade the new regulations. They objected to the renewal of an unprecedented seventy-five licences.

On 14 February new restrictions came into force: pubs could open for the sale of alcohol only between 12.00 and 2.30 pm and 6.30 and 9.30 pm, except on Sundays, when they closed at 9.00 pm. To make matters worse, the strength of spirits was to be reduced by 10 degrees. One result of this was a marked reduction in the numbers arrested for drink related offences. Paradoxically, Inland Revenue returns suggest there was no reduction in the amount people were drinking. Some pubs, however, suffered greatly and a number in the business centre of the city resorted to desperate measures: they began selling tea, coffee and soft drinks. One licensee, however, was upbeat: 'I don't see why a public house run on teetotal lines for part of the day should not do fairly well,' he said. Like many others, this landlord was busy stocking up with crockery, tea and coffee. Notices outside the city's famed drinking dens, 'Open for Tea and Coffee', raised wry smiles and were whisked away on the stroke of midday. Many former tipplers developed a taste for meat extract drinks, while numerous wags bemoaned the fact that the 'no treating' rule was a cruel blow to those who had imbibed at the expense of others all their lives.

By March 1916 Manchester publicans were so beleaguered that they began to see behind the restrictions imposed on them the sinister hand of the prohibitionist. In the annual report of the Council of Manchester, Salford and District Licensed Victuallers' and Retailers' Association, they spoke of a policy of 'creeping teetotalism' masquerading as patriotism. This was, they believed, solely designed to damage the trade without in any way advancing the war effort. This view seems to be supported by the alarming rate at which pubs were closing. Prohibitionists certainly regarded the war as an opportunity to advance their agenda. In December the Strength of Britain Movement launched a recruitment campaign that included extensive newspaper adverting, coupled with a demand for prohibition.

Many, however, felt that Manchester had too many pubs. In March 1916 there were still 2,319 licenses in the city; or one drinking establishment for every 325 people including women and children. Magistrates issued a stern warning to parents who left their children outside pubs that if this resulted in suffering they would be sent to prison. Yet it had to be admitted that once more the number of arrests for drunkenness was falling and was now half that before the introduction of the most recent restrictions.

Among those too poor to visit pubs were many members of the 'respectable middle class'. In March 1916 the city's teachers appealed to the education committee for an immediate pay rise. Approximately 700 were paid between £50 and £75 a year, or between 19/- and 27/6d a week, at a time when a female tram driver received 22/- a week. Road sweepers received a minimum of 26/- a week plus a war bonus of 2/-, as did dustmen, whereas uncertified women teachers received between 17/- and 27/- a week and men 21/- to 35/-. Certified women teachers received between £75 and £130 a year and men between £90 and £150. Though it was clear that many teachers were leaving for other, better paid, work, the City Council refused to consider their request.

At the end of the year the teachers were once more in the news as it became clear that education in the city was in crisis. Four thousand teachers from Manchester and Salford applied for a rise of £20 a year, pointing out that that teachers' pay in the twin cities was considerably behind that of other areas, teachers were leaving the profession in great numbers and applications for teaching posts had recently fallen by two thirds. Teachers, then as now, enjoyed little public sympathy.

The same applied to the Irish nationalist rebels; the majority of the city's non-Irish population regarded them as traitors. The city's large Irish population was as dismayed as everyone else when on Tuesday, 25 April news of the Easter Rising in Dublin reached Britain. Local newspapers described events as 'disturbances' and told of the rebels seizing the General Post Office. Much local coverage focused on the capture of the 'notorious' Roger Casement while attempting to land arms on the west coast of Ireland. The end of the rising was reported on 1 May. Subsequently local papers gave scant coverage of the execution of the leaders, the imprisonment of seventy-nine and the deportation of over 1,700 rebels.

Roger Casement, the former senior member of the British consular service, who was hanged on 3 August, attracted most press venom. The feeling of most Mancunians was that Ireland was full of shirkers whose antipathy to British interests was such that they had conspired with her enemies in her hour of greatest need. Resentment towards the Irish in the city was intense, though there is no record of it resulting in inter-communal violence.

Far more coverage was devoted to the major battles of the year. From 3 June details of the Battle of Jutland – the greatest sea battle of the War – appeared in local papers. The city took a keen interest in naval affairs because Manchester had a proud record of recruitment to maritime service.

Many of the brightest and best products of the city's industrial schools were scattered throughout the navy but were particularly concentrated in the North Sea Fleet, which had been at the heart of the battle. Since the war began at least 130 products of the Ardwick and St Joseph industrial schools had joined the navy. One of these, Jack Shaw of the

Invincible, had carried the green flag at the head of the St Joseph's pipers in the Whit Friday procession of 1914. Another St Joseph's boy, Harry Kenny, was aboard the *Black Prince*. Both were sunk.

In the following days news of other vessels came through: the *Indefatigable* was lost – no survivors; of the thousand hands aboard the *Queen Mary*, seven survived. Concerned relatives queued at the navy recruitment office on Deansgate, anxious for news of their loved ones. One man, described as 'a big strapping chap with *INDEFATIGABLE* on a band on his round hat' was clearly distressed. He had been on extended leave due to his father's illness and was clearly distraught at the prospect of having lost mates.

Of even greater impact on Manchester were events on the Somme. The *Picture House*, Oxford Road, became the first to show the film *The Battle of the Somme*, which was immensely popular in the city and played to full houses every night of its long run. At the same time details of the casualties began to come through – first a trickle and then an inundation. They took up an enormous amount of space in the local newspapers and for many in the city it became impossible to read them without finding the name of someone they knew. Everyone, it seemed, wore mourning. 'Black, black, black everywhere', one man recalled.

Manchester men played a key role on the Somme. Unlike 4th Manchester, who achieved its objective with relatively light casualties, the 1st and 2nd Battalions suffered dreadful losses. It was, however, the 7th Manchester's attack on Danzig Alley that caused

This map from the Official History identifies the positions assaulted by the 5th, 6th and 7th City Battalions during the events of 1st July, 1916.

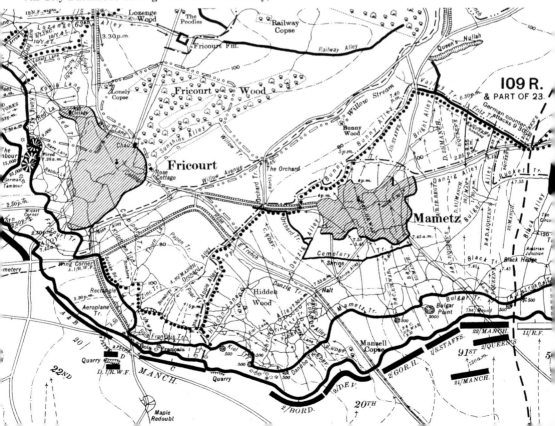

Tiny figures can be clearly seen against the chalk spoil as the 7th Divisions assault battalions, the 7th City Battalion, the 22nd Manchesters, and the 1st South Staffordshires move forwards towards Mametz. Taylor Library

it to suffer almost 500 casualties, more than any other Pals' Battalion on the opening day of the Battle. The next day 1st and 2nd City Battalions took the brunt of a ferocious counter-attack and heavy shelling. However, 19th Manchesters, on the first day of the Somme, in what was their first significant action, achieved a brilliant success.

Two days after the initial attack, Albert Andrews, a Manchester Pal, wrote home after spending the day burying his dead comrades: 'This was when we realised the cost of the victory. Burying your own lads is not a job I want again.'

At home, too, the reality was beginning to emerge. For the first time Kitchener's New Army had been used en masse and the results were dreadful. The first day of the Somme was the bloodiest day in the history of the British army. Within a week the

The attack on Danzig Alley left the 7th City Battalion with more casualties than any other Manchester Pals unit on 1 July. Taylor Library

Manchester Evening News's headline went from, 'Kitchener's Boys: New Armies Make Good' to 'Heavy Toll of the City Units'. The great disadvantage of the pals' battalions dawned on the public as bereavement blighted huge swathes of the city.

In the weeks that followed countless Manchester homes received the dreaded buff envelope, stamped with OHMS. 8-year-old Dennis Gilfeather remembers the day the postman knocked on their door. 'It was a Saturday morning and my mum was feeding us. The baby was in the high chair and she was serving out when there was a knock at the door. I remember her slight annoyance at the disruption as she went to answer it. I saw her open the door and take the letter. She tore it open, her hands were shaking. Then she read it and collapsed on the floor.'

Bereavement permeated every facet of the city's life for the remainder of 1916. As the year drew to a close the weather began to improve and there was a last-minute rush to the shops. Shopkeepers reported that though that, although there was a brisk demand for extravagantly priced boxes of chocolate, most were spending their money on practicalities. A new type of customer, the working class, appeared and spent heavily despite the high prices. In the city's picture palaces, *Maid of the Mountain* played to packed and enthusiastic houses while those who travelled to be with family were perhaps happy they had done so when they learnt that new restrictions on travel were to be introduced in the new year, with a twenty five per cent reduction in the number of trains leaving Central Station. Not only would it be no longer possible to travel directly to Southport but the number of trains to Cheshire destinations was greatly reduced.

As the year drew to a close, the city was enveloped in impenetrable fog. It was the foggiest winter on record.

Chapter 4

1917: Endurance

'I've never seen the place look so bare.'

Headless corpses were among the broken bodies littering the streets. Men and women, some on fire, ran screaming in terror while others scuttled out of the town, abandoning their homes and fleeing for the safety of the moors.

THIS HAPPENED NOT in some unfortunate town on the Western Front as it was shelled by heavy artillery but in Ashton-under-Lyne, on the edge of Manchester.

Manchester's greatest industrial disaster took place on 13 June when an explosion at the Hooley Hill Rubber and Chemical Works killed forty-one and injured hundreds. The factory was producing TNT for the government. The explosion and subsequent fires destroyed two thousand homes.

The disaster began with a fire in the William Street section of the factory which spread and led to an explosion which shook buildings three miles away, demolishing over one hundred nearby cottages, workshops and other structures. In the words of one local newspaper, the factory itself was 'blown to atoms'. Two nearby gasometers caught fire and rumours of a second explosion caused panic as hundreds fled for the open country of Ashton Moss, carrying what they could of their belongings. Of the 150 workers on the night shift, four miraculously survived injury. Many of those in hospital remained gravely injured and three died almost immediately.

Separated from the factory by a canal, the Bridge End Mill caught fire and burnt to the ground, as did Messrs Clayton, hay and straw merchant, almost a mile away. Hardly a pane of glass in the town survived and the damage to local cotton mills meant that hundreds of workers were made idle. The force of the explosion was such that a railway worker mending the track nearby was decapitated.

There were plenty consumed by ghoulish curiosity and in the following days thousands poured into the town to witness the extent of the devastation. A relief fund was immediately launched and raised £1,900 within five days of the disaster.

Perhaps more than any other single incident, the explosion impressed on the city the extent to which the war had come to dominate every facet of life. It was now all-pervasive. Many diarists testify that even in sleep it was impossible to escape it. The war was enveloping everything, turning the city in on itself.

Even temporary physical escape was becoming impossible. The number of passenger trains was shrinking and those that remained were much slower; many stations were closed; luggage was restricted and fares increased by fifty per cent. Unsurprisingly, travellers reported appalling conditions, in which sixteen people were crammed into a carriage intended for six and coaches meant to carry 600 packed to bursting with over a 1,000 sweating commuters. On the first Sunday of the year those who had used some of the limited services to get out into the countryside were forced to walk long distances home when several trains failed to materialise.

In March the number of suburban trains was again reduced and late evening services ended. The situation for Easter holiday makers, hoping to get away for one of the coldest Easters on record, was worse than ever. Higher fares and fewer trains were bad enough, but new regulations meant that tickets could be bought only on the day of travel from the railway ticket office and were limited by the reduced space available. North easterly gales deterred football fans from attending games. The weather was so inclement that the customary Whit processions and children's outings were cancelled.

Fewer were taking solace in drink: from 9,053 arrests for alcohol-related offences in 1913, the figure fell to 3,052 in 1916. The reason is not hard to find: the opportunities to drink were continuing to shrink. The Food Controller announced that from 1 April beer production would fall by a further thirty per cent, thus reducing it to half the pre-war level. This would, he assured irate drinkers, make available huge quantities of barley, sugar and cattle food.

The Manchester brewers were further beleaguered by the activities of the temperance lobby and felt compelled to strike back. In March they launched a massive advertising campaign and, like their opponents, latched onto the food issue, claiming that beer is not only a food but also helps with shortages as ' it makes solid food more easily assimilated and so less of it is needed for nutrition'. Yet, later in the month, there was widespread consternation in the city's pubs: the vexed drinker had now to contend with a scarcity of beer and consequent price rises.

By July licensees felt that concerted action against creeping state control was essential. They met in enormous numbers at Houldsworth Hall and asserted their opposition to government control. Yet their worst fears were realised when the Food Controller instructed brewers to reduce the price of a pint to no more than 4d or 5d depending on its alcoholic content. One reason for this directive was to attract people away from spirits, the sale of which had greatly increased since the start of the war and which the authorities deemed more damaging than beer to health and war production.

Together with the fall in drunkenness there was a parallel fall in crime generally, though a major exception was bigamy. But for an excellent war record Henry Coghill would have received a more severe sentence than eighteen months imprisonment when he was convicted at the Spring Assizes of marrying bigamously; not once, but twice. Sarah Marron, a rag sorter, took advantage of her husband's service at the front to enter into a bigamous marriage. She received only three months.

Bigamists were still to the fore when the Winter Assizes opened in November: the twenty charged with the offence made up almost half the total number of cases. Most were soldiers or the wives of soldiers. What appalled Mr Justice Shearman was that several bigamists were motivated not by unwise love but by the desire to claim additional army separation allowance.

Those women who were properly entitled to the separation allowance were finding that rising food prices were continuing to erode its value. The government feared that lack of food threatened civilian morale more than anything else, which is why it intervened to fix the price of milk. However, some of the means by which the Food

Controller sought to avoid shortages served only to antagonise many. For instance, in February he told the British people, 'Economy is not only a patriotic duty but a necessity'. He went on to remind heads of households that they should limit their weekly purchases so that each member of the family ate no more than 4lb of bread, 2¼lb of meat and ¾ lb of sugar. One woman a local paper interviewed in a butcher's was buying her weekly ration of 3lb of meat for herself and eight children. She was indignant that people who for a long time had lived largely on bread and margarine were now being asked to eat even less. Few people, she said, had been able to get ¾ lb of sugar for several months and many people had been without any for far longer.

Complaints about bread were now a staple of everyday conversation and reached a peak of discontent during the summer. It was not simply less palatable than previously – many claimed it was also less nourishing. Millers were allowed to put into flour up to ten per cent of ingredients other than wheat. The variation in taste – one week passable, the next inedible – was also a cause of complaint. From early September the quality did improve slightly as the government allowed millers to use low-grade Manitoba wheat in place of maize. By then, however, white bread had disappeared from the shops.

With German U-boats trying to sink every cargo ship bound for Britain, food supplies were being choked off and in 1917 fear of starvation came to underpin every other concern. In 1914 Britain imported two-thirds of calories consumed and by April 1917 there were no more than a couple of weeks' food supplies left.

The poor suffered most, as the bread, which was such an essential part of their diet, depended on imported wheat. For such people, meat of any type was a luxury and hunger now became an unremarked part of everyday life.

More than anything else it was with regard to food that working class people felt they were being treated unfairly and that others were not shouldering their fair share of the burden. It was a major factor contributing to an 'us and them' attitude, as it was widely believed that shops in middle-class areas were well stocked and that it was only in poor areas that people queued for their food. Many middle class families retained their domestic help – as late as 1917 there were still 1,250,000 British women in service – the chief advantage of which was having someone to queue for food.

To make up for the food that was ending up at the bottom of the Atlantic, the city authorities made enormous efforts to encourage Mancunians to grow their own. In January the Manchester Foodstuffs Special Committee announced that it was planting an additional 290 acres of potatoes and oats. In late January it announced a series of lectures on rearing poultry according to the 'intensive system'. Neither strategy was advanced by the prolonged cold weather, making it the coldest January for many years. On the night of 30 January the temperature was 20.4 degrees Fahrenheit, or 11 degrees of frost. The snow and fog continued into early February. An epidemic of frozen pipes struck the city on 5 February, when the temperature fell to a record low for the city centre, 11 degrees Fahrenheit. The extreme cold took its toll on an exhausted and undernourished population: almost three hundred tram conductors and drivers were absent through illness on a single day. As late as 9 March there were successive evenings when there were 13 degrees of frost.

By the middle of February people were speaking of a 'potato famine' in Manchester and once more the suppliers were blamed for holding back stocks in order to raise prices. Within a few days the threat of government intervention seemed to have alleviated the problem, as traders in Smithfield Market reported more potatoes were available. But at the end of March even hospitals could not get the potatoes they needed and they were virtually impossible to find in poor areas. One greengrocer on Stretford Road, who had a good supply, rationed them to a maximum of 4lb per customer, only to find that people from all over the area were drawn by the news; he soon had a queue 250 yards long.

The sugar problem was getting worse too. It was almost impossible to find a grocer prepared to sell other than to good customers spending a substantial amount. In the poor areas of the city, such as Ancoats and Hulme, it was necessary to spend at least 1/6d in order to get two ounces of sugar which cost a penny. Poor people were therefore paying 8d for a pound for sugar, which had cost 2d before the war. This particular shortage was regarded by many as a major reason for much of the sickness which was common among children in poor areas. One lady social worker remarked that 'the children of the poorer districts of Manchester are much more anaemic and debilitated than they were in peace time. It is obvious that they are not getting the proper amount of food.' The infant mortality figures, which show an increase in some of the poorer areas, support these opinions. One doctor stated that 'there is no doubt that there is much suffering and sickness among children because of their poor food'.

By the end of February the potato shortage was still a problem and several of the Smithfield traders specialising in chip potatoes had gone out of business. There was an embargo on the import of Irish potatoes and this made matters worse and increased public annoyance, as rumours were circulating to the effects that enormous stocks of Irish potatoes were being unnecessarily delayed by the Department of Agriculture.

In early March the courts cracked down on potato dealers, who were among the most unpopular men in the city. Three were fined £2 and three £5 for charging excessive prices. By the end of the month merchants had virtually no potatoes to sell at any price. One housewife who had five soldiers billeted on her was able to obtain only 5lb a week.

It's hardly surprising that by the beginning of March the Manchester Corporation Foodstuffs Committee had received 500 applications for allotments. By the end of the summer 3,000 Corporation plots were under cultivation and the authorities were congratulating the novice growers on how well the city had risen to the challenge. Some councillors – on the basis of what evidence is not clear – claimed that Manchester's response was superior to that of any other city. Their highest praise was for the allotments created on Princess Road on former football fields, on Sunderland Street in Harphurhey and on French Barn Street. Many gardeners' huts on Princess Road were curtained, with interiors as good as any well-maintained home. The Sunderland Street allotments were on ground that had once been a cinder tip and one of the most unsightly spots in the entire city. The transformation wrought in these places inspired many working men to become expert growers in a short time.

Expert or not, there was little anyone could do about the weather. August 1917 was one of the wettest the city had ever experienced: it rained on twenty-six days. By September it was still raining and the corn crop was threatened.

In September the Princess Road allotment holders staged a show to encourage more people to grow their own vegetables. The president of the Moss Side Allotment Holders' Society, Mr Matthewson Watson, boasted that the area had more allotments than anywhere in Britain; they produced giant marrows, carrots, turnips and every vegetable imaginable, yet the familiar potato remained the pride of the show.

Many of those who were unable to grow their own blamed the farmers for shortages, claiming that they found it more profitable to sell their stock directly to restaurants and retailers prepared to pay a premium. Others blamed hoarders, while the government put the onus on the public to exercise voluntary restraint. Government research showed that the vast majority of the city's families did their best to conform to government requests. For the poor, the very idea of restraint was nonsense, as one diarist remembers that bread and 'scrape' was his family's standard breakfast, while potatoes and bread – perhaps with some dripping – was usually their main meal. Though many retailers dreaded the prospect of rationing, Mr James Kendall of the Manchester, Salford and District Grocers' Association, saw no alternative and believed that it 'is what is wanted to make people understand the necessity of some sacrifice'. But, he stressed, no scheme, not even rationing, would work if the government did not solve the supply problem. Already it was commonplace for shops to run out of basic food items.

Those who had taken to growing their own food were continually hampered by the bad weather. In the early days of April the city was hit by blizzards, four inches of snow and 10 degrees of frost. Local dignitaries were pushing the new Food Economy Campaign Handbook and reminding people that 'a victory in the present terrible struggle now depends upon our women'.

In May bread again became the focus of concerns. By this time maize, barley and rice were being used to supplement wheat and the resultant colour, texture and taste were to the liking of few. One housewife complained that it was often inedible and was 'very dark, heavy and tasted of yeast'. Later various amounts of potato were added, which only increased complaints about the 'war loaf' or 'black loaf', which became progressively more spongy and malodorous. The advantage of this for underfed children was that they waited outside factories at closing time and begged the workers to give them the remains of uneaten lunches.

In May it was the soaring price of meat that was the major cause of complaint. In a single week the price of mutton increased by 4d a pound and chops reached the outrageous price of 2/- a pound. The bad weather, apparently, had slowed the growth of sheep and many were not yet ready for slaughter. Some, of course, were inclined to blame the butchers, who claimed that they too were suffering and that many of them were being forced out of business, having actually lost money during 1916. Local restrictions reduced supplies to hotels and restaurants to seventy-five per cent of their needs and by September it was clear that control orders were having very little effect on prices, which continued to rise as many retailers simply ignored them.

On 17 October papers reported that meat stocks in the city were sufficient for no more than two days.

Towards the end of the year the steady trickle of letters to the newspapers complaining of food profiteers exploiting the public became a torrent. The city's Director of Food Economy, Mr Yapp, came in for a great deal of irate criticism when he admonished the public for eating too much and exhorted manual labourers to eat no more than eight pounds of bread and two pounds of meat a week. Incensed housewives berated his ignorance of the realities of the food situation, complaining that no working man could afford that amount of meat. In addition, the price of fish was so high that it was no longer a practical alternative for those who could not afford meat.

The length of queues for food remained a major source of annoyance. By December it was extremely difficult to obtain meat and queues for tea and margarine were long. This was a cause of great hardship for the poor and support for rationing was now overwhelming. It finally arrived with the announcement on Christmas Eve that it was to be administered by the Local Food Control Committee, which was to meet immediately to decide how best to operate the scheme.

But food was not the only necessity in short supply. Though working class people of all ages were dependent on second hand clothes, increases in the price of new garments inevitably affected them too. The ubiquitous pre-war three guinea suit, so beloved of the middle class, disappeared, as such a suit now cost a minimum of £4. Suit material was in short supply and many tailors had great difficulty replenishing stocks. In 1917 the Garment Workers' Union and the Middleman's Society, whose members were notoriously poorly paid, demanded an increase on the price paid for making up garments. The bosses resisted on the grounds that the civilian market was shrinking and the shortage of materials was already forcing up prices.

The problem of rising rents surfaced in August 1917. Despite the Rents Restriction Act of 1915 – which decreed that the standard rent was that paid at the outbreak of war and that any increases had to be justified in terms of structural alterations, increased property taxes or water charges – many landlords had tried to take advantage of the shortage of accommodation to increase rents. In August many tenants, organised in the Local Tenants' Defence Association, refused to pay increases and in many cases actually secured the return of increases already paid. One local newspaper pointed out that according to the Act, the largest valid increase since 1914 was 2½d a week in north Manchester and that there was no justification for any increase in the south of the city.

As for the few luxuries left to the poor, the Budget of May did nothing to help them. Further taxes on entertainment and tobacco put 4d on the price of a shilling music hall ticket and a penny on a pack of ten cigarettes. All these factors put more pressure on wages and ensured that the demand for pay rises would continue.

Industrial relations continued to deteriorate and 1917 was the worst year for strikes since the war began. One factor was the introduction of conscription. Other factors were dilution – the use of unskilled workers to perform tasks previously the preserve of craftsmen – the shrinking of wage differentials, food prices, the general rise in the cost of living and fuel discontent.

In a continuing wages dispute, the spinners rejected an offer of ten per cent, while on 1 April the engineers received an additional 5/- a week bonus. In May 30,000 engineers in south Lancashire went on strike because the Munitions Department continued to insist that the unskilled should be allowed to perform tasks traditionally the preserve of craftsmen. In July the cotton spinners demanded a thirty per cent rise. But the problems affecting the cotton industry were more complex. Shortage of raw cotton led, in

September, to the Cotton Control Board imposing production restrictions and employers' levies to alleviate the suffering of those put out of work. The system was initially planned to run for three months, by which time it was hoped supplies would improve; but by October there was widespread unemployment in the cotton industry.

At the end of March the city's carters threatened to strike. In May, 600 employees of the Co-Operative Wholesale Society in Eccles went on strike. The Amalgamated Society of Engineers and Allied Trades, whose members had been on strike for a week, held their conference in Manchester and voted to return to work. The employers exacerbated the situation by issuing a statement claiming that all those who failed to return were betraying the men at the front. In fact, only fifty per cent returned as agreed, the rest drifting back piecemeal.

The disgruntlement among engineers was in part political. As on Clydeside, the shop stewards' committees had become a major force in the industry and often operated in open opposition to the union's executive committees, many of which had lost the allegiance of their members as it was widely felt that they had not addressed workers' grievances. The problem of the dilution of labour was a festering grievance, poisoning relations. Added to this was the abolition of the trade card system, which gave those working in key industries exemption from military service. The new system of exempted professions applied to fewer workers.

On Monday 18 May the government took a risky decision: police arrested the engineers' leaders in Manchester and whisked them to London, where they were joined by their colleagues who had been arrested in Sheffield and the capital. The key figures from Manchester were George Peat, of Abbey Hey Lane, Gorton and P.H. Kealey, of Byer Street, Gorton, who were charged with 'impeding the supply of weapons'. The reaction of the union executive committee was to order its members to return to work while negotiations continued through the established channels. The Manchester men responded by returning in large numbers, though it seems that this was in no small part due to the influence of the shop stewards who spoke to the men at a mass meeting and recommended a resumption of work. It seems the engineers now expected the arrested men to be released. This did not occur and when instead they were brought before Bow Street magistrates, the Attorney General stated that all had signed an undertaking to abide by an agreement between the Amalgamated Society of Engineers and the government. The charges were then withdrawn, though with a warning that those involved in further disruption would henceforward be prosecuted. Though the Liverpool engineers remained on strike, a major confrontation in Manchester had been avoided.

On 8 August Manchester's dockers refused to work with non-union men -- specifically two men who refused to join the union. The use of non-union labour had been a festering sore for years. Mr Blundell, the union spokesman, asserted that despite this action the dockers had proved themselves 'as loyal and as patriotic as any other class of workmen'.

Perhaps the most incendiary strike of all was that of the city tram workers, who on 26 June and in defiance of their union's recommendation, initiated a work to rule. The public, however, was less than sympathetic and intensely annoyed by the inconvenience caused. It was not long before annoyance turned to rage. In Gorton, men leaving a munitions factory after work overpowered the crew of a tram and drove it off. There were many altercations between staff and travellers, often arising from the refusal of travellers to accept that trams were full when so informed by female conductors. This frequently led to a standoff: staff refused to move the tram because it was over full while passengers refuse to get off. In the words of one account, 'for many hours altercations continued and in many cases all restraint of temper and language was absent. In many of the resulting disputes blows were exchanged.' In other cases, drivers refused to stop at designated stops, leaving fuming commuters shaking their fists in impotent rage.

On the night of 4 July the tram workers held a midnight meeting at which they rejected the exhortations of their union leaders to resume normal working and instead voted to go on strike the following night unless the Tramways Committee increased its previous offer of 2/6 a week rise. Such a stoppage threatened a calamitous effect on every aspect of industrial production, especially munitions.

The intensity of public feeling was made clear at the City Police Court on 6 July, when Mary Gaskell of Swinton was fined 10/- and 10/6 advocate's fee for assaulting Sarah Jane Yates, a tram guard. She was also fined an additional 5/6 for using offensive language. In her defence Mrs Gaskell said she had been driven to it by the flirtatious manner in which the guard had spoken to her husband. At the same hearing a police superintendent stood accused of assaulting another female guard. That case was dismissed.

At this stage, just as an all-out strike was imminent, the Labour Ministry announced that a tram strike was illegal and those involved would be arrested under the Munitions of War Act. The Permanent Secretary to the Ministry, Sir David Shakleton, undertook to arbitrate and promised a decision within fourteen days. Despite a ballot in favour of strike action, normal working was resumed. Eventually, on 11 July, the tram workers were given a bonus of 2/6. This was far below their expectations but they felt that, having given their word to accept arbitration, they were honour bound to remain at work.

The parlous state of industrial relations now threatened the entire war effort. At the end of July Judge Parry was in Manchester, conducting an inquiry into the situation. Mr Purcell, chairman of the Trades Council, made a statement with which no one could disagree: prices had been locked into an upward trajectory for many years and the impact of the war meant workers were finding it extremely difficult to feed their families. On top of this fundamental problem, numerous other complaints were overlaid: the restrictions on alcohol, the industrial fatigue that inevitably arises when workers are working over the entire weekend as well as long hours during the week, and the demoralising effects of increasing pressure to work faster.

Conditions in the factories were also causing a generalised sense of grievance: the imposition of quasi-judicial hearings to maintain discipline, the refusal of the management to address complaints, the government's continued insistence on the dilution of skilled labour, the frequent refusal of employers to issue leaving certificates and the appointment of arbiters to industrial disputes who lacked understanding of the issues involved, all antagonised workers. The dilution issue was an continuing cause of conflict between workers and management. The unions had acceded to it in order to increase arms production. However, many companies also continued with commercial work and sought to introduce it there as well. As a consequence of this the position of militants in the industry was strengthened, as many men felt that bosses were seeking to undermine hard earned working agreements on which their status as skilled workers depended.

The food problem was also having a major impact on industrial relations. At the most generous estimate the wages of manual workers had increased by fifty per cent since the outbreak of war while food prices had risen by 105 per cent. All the restrictions on food in reality applied only to the poor: those with money could still obtain anything they wanted. Unfair distribution of essentials was corroding morale and fostering pervasive disgruntlement.

Meanwhile, military developments were mixed. News in early April that the USA had joined the Allies gave the city a great boost. Local papers reported that the American government planned to send its entire force to bolster the Western Front. In tribute to the new allies, the Town Hall flew the American flag on 4 July. The more perceptive, however, realised that with the Russian collapse in November, the entire strength of the German army could now be brought to bear on the Western Front.

The same month the story that the Germans were operating a corpse factory in which the bodies of soldiers were rendered down for their fat and used for munitions and animal feed appeared in the local newspapers. The Manchester papers were particularly keen on stories about the Kaiser's poor health. In March he was, reportedly, dying of Bright's disease while going insane.

War weariness showed itself in antagonism to all those perceived as shirking their duty in the national cause. Foremost among these were the Irish. The rising of 1916 led to a great deal of anti-Irish antagonism, a sentiment which, together with its concomitant anti-Catholic bigotry, was prevalent in certain quarters of the city. In July workers at a large chemical plant refused to work with Irishmen, who consequently were given a week's notice and told to return home. As the men, about 200 in total, entrained for Dublin at Exchange Station, they were met by a hostile crowd waving flags and singing patriotic songs. The police attended in great numbers as the crowd became increasingly vociferous. Many of the Irishmen were of military age but all refused to join up and proclaimed their support for the IRA.

Similarly, pacifists, regarded as cowards who were betraying the men at the front, continued as the objects of popular odium. The Milton House Committee refused to allow the Hall to be used for a meeting of the Soldiers' and Workmen's Council, which was in fact a pacifist organization. In order to make the organisation's nature clear to all, the Manchester and Salford Sailors' and Soldiers' Federation posted a resolution repudiating the Council.

On 11 August pacifists from Lancashire, Cheshire and North Wales met at Stockport Labour Church, Hillgate. The principal speakers were Mr W.C. Anderson MP and Mr Arthur Williams of the Transport Workers. Admission was by invitation only but news of the event leaked out and the delegates were met by members of the British Workers' League, who had recently broken up a similar meeting in Stephenson Square. On this occasion 'Traitors' Peace Meeting' was scrawled on the pavement in large letters. Soon a large crowd gathered at the entrance where Mr J.H. Pendlebury, of the British Workers'

AISLE H. MACHINE SHOP
WESTINGHOUSE WORKS

Westinghouse Machine shop, one of the city's major producers of war materials.
Mark Flynn Postcards

League, mounted a chair and proceeded to denounce all pacifists as cowards and traitors. Plain clothes police interfered only when a butcher's cart found the crowd was blocking the road. Mr Pendlebury obligingly moved his chair.

On 8 September the police banned another pacifist demonstration planned for Stephenson Square. The organizers were 'well known women social and political workers', including Mrs Philip Snowden – the wife of a leading Labour politician – and Mrs Margaret Ashton. An enormous crowd gathered for the event but it soon became clear that most were there with the intention of disrupting the meeting, including many wounded soldiers who were determined to hold an anti-pacifist protest. As the meeting was about to start it became clear that there was going to be trouble and Superintendent Gilmour, at the head of a large body of police, cancelled proceedings. The police were cheered but the crowd's attitude towards the organizers was such that they decided to take refuge in Newton Street police station.

However, a number of events alleviated the gloom and brought people together. George V and Queen Mary visited the city on 15 and 16 May. Though the weather was as cold as it had been for most of the year, exuberant crowds lined the route, glad of the colour and spectacle of the occasion in what seemed to be a relentless round of hardship and shortages. The king visited the Westinghouse plant at Old Trafford, which was synonymous with the most advanced electrical technology of the day, while Queen Mary spent her time at the Royal Infirmary and with the 5,000 soldiers convalescing in Heaton Park. She later went to a munitions factory and the Whitworth Street Hospital, one of the country's biggest clearing stations for wounded soldiers. The visit was marked by an air of informality – the royal couple were relaxed and delighted by the warmth of the people they met.

The following month Private George Stringer, proudly displaying his VC, arrived home to a tumultuous reception, including a civil reception in Albert Square. The following day saw a round of visits, including his old school, the Albert Memorial School, Miles Platting and his former place of work, Kerr & Hoegger, where he was a bleacher.

In July it was announced that horse racing would resume and there would be forty days racing throughout the country from August, including events at Castle Irwell on 4 and 6 August and the November Handicap on the 17th of the month. Better still, on 5 July, the local newspapers announced the government was to allow more beer to be brewed.

Yet as what was to be the final Christmas of the war approached there was little

Ducie Avenue Military Hospital, one of the many schools adapted for the treatment of wounded soldiers. Rusholme Archives

evidence of good cheer. The books and toys that were available were extremely costly. Many of the foods associated with Christmas were prohibitively expensive or else unobtainable at any price. In the week before Christmas, Shudehill, the area around Smithfield Market, where in previous Christmases the pavements were packed with shoppers, was virtually deserted. Oranges were few and even English apples, one of the few fruits available, were very dear. Stallholders could not even hold out the hope of

Wounded soldiers and their nurses in a Victoria Park Red Cross hospital.
Rusholme Archives

VICTORIA PARK ~ MANCHESTER · RED
PHOTO BY WARD 249 OxFoRD Rd M

obtaining nuts or bananas. A few English grapes were for sale but at prices that made them accessible to only the affluent. Similarly, Norfolk turkey cost 2/6 a pound, almost twice the price of the previous Christmas.

The effect of this on the poor who hoped to have fowl as a special treat at this time of the year was to make that wish impossible. Tomatoes were fetching a record wholesale price of 1/3 a pound. There was neither holly nor mistletoe available and few Christmas

trees. The shortage of meat was such that butchers were unable to mount displays in their windows and were selling only to loyal customers. They were unanimous in saying that it is impossible for them to buy at prices which allowed them to sell in accordance with the Price Controller's limits. As one market stallholder said, 'In all my thirty years' experience, I've never seen the place look so bare'.

The length of queues grew to a bewildering extent, especially in poorer parts of the city. Three days before Christmas a grocer's on the corner of St Mary's Gate and Deansgate attracted a queue that stretched down Deansgate beyond Exchange Street – at least a thousand people – even before it opened. The shop was one of the few in the city with margarine. The police arrived, though in truth there was little need for them: the mood was one of docile resignation.

Resignation to hardship was also the attitude of the poor. A spokesman for the Wood Street Mission said that the numbers applying for help were greater than ever and offered the dire warning that 'to these the approach of winter with today's prices for foodstuffs is likely to lead to starvation, whilst clothing and footwear are already an impossibility in many houses. The mothers in these homes bear their burdens ungrudgingly, knowing that they are doing their bit in the service of the nation.'

Even the mothers' stoicism was not enough to meet the growing need. At least one local newspaper believed that communal food kitchens were essential if many more people were not to go hungry. It was not even possible to drown one's sorrows – beer was so scarce in the city that many brewers were rationing their pubs. Hardy Crown Brewery's 108 pubs were open only at the weekend and others introduced restricted hours.

The abiding image of 1917 was that of badly clothed women queuing in the raw, cold morning in the hope of getting a little margarine. Inconvenience and discomfort were not the worst effects of this: the city coroner, Mr Sellars, surmised that the increase in child fatalities was a result of mothers spending so much time queuing for food.

Chapter Five

1918: The End

'With youth has gone much of the effervescence, the heedless gaiety.'

A FIGHTER IS great not because he is never knocked down but because when he is and when he has no power in his legs, when his arms are too heavy to lift and his senses blurred with pain, he rises, and, drawing from some unknown resource, claws his way back into contention. The capacity to endure beyond pain, to bear beyond hope and to continue doing what is insufferable is the fortitude that wins wars. Nowhere was this more evident than in Manchester during 1918, when it seemed that a succession of scourgings must surely break the people's will.

Most terrible of all was the spectre of hunger that haunted every house in the city and threatened to disrupt the entire war effort. Hunger was a nagging preoccupation, a constant ache, filling every waking moment in the early months of 1918.

On 16 January two thousand munitions workers left their factories in Openshaw and Gorton and, cheered along their way by women queuing for food, marched into Albert Square, demanding an end to food shortages and long queues. A further 2,000 from all over the city joined them in the city centre. The Lord Mayor came out to speak to them and later received a deputation, which presented a petition. The leaders of the deputation warned that 'the people could not stand the conditions much longer'. The Lord Mayor, supported by Daniel McCabe, chairman of the Food Control Committee, expressed his deepest sympathy and assured the men that everything possible was being done to improve the situation. At this point the crowd became fractious, shouting in response to the Mayor's words, 'No!' 'No!' Yet when the Chief Constable, Mr Peacock, advised them to return to work immediately while their deputation went into the Town Hall, they did so with little grumbling.

Mr J. Shaw, head of the deputation, stressed that it was the unfairness of food distribution that was intolerable and was making the situation far worse than it need be. Many of the workers, he said, were reduced to living on little other than bread and jam and their patience was running out. 'The men would not wait,' he said, 'as they are tired of going home and finding their women in tears because, despite queuing all day, they could get no food.' Finally, Shaw added something that must have alarmed the Mayor: 'If nothing is done to remedy the state of affairs, the workers' committees would not be responsible for anything happening in the [work]shops. How can the workers be expected to work fourteen hours a day without proper food?'

Another member of the delegation, Mr Monroe, said, 'There is a limit to human endurance and the workers have reached that limit.' Then, in case the import of his colleague's words had not been understood, he added that he 'was prepared to take part in a revolution if something is not done soon'.

One of the women on the delegation spoke movingly of the plight of solders' wives who, after a day's work, go to the shops only to discover the shelves bare.

Local papers carried details of how the rationing system would work when it eventually came into effect. The weekly ration would guarantee each person four ounces of butter or margarine and one and a half ounces of tea. In order to get this entitlement it was first necessary for the housewife to register with a grocer who would supply her food. Meanwhile, to avoid queues the Food Control Committee commandeered margarine and distributed it around the city to seventy small grocers. But this did nothing to help the meat situation, as many butchers had nothing to sell and those who did were immediately descended on by hundreds of women.

On 17 January the workers of the principal Trafford Park companies, backed by the Manchester and Salford Trade Council, called for a strike against the Food Control Committee. But not everyone blamed the Committee. Many said shortages were partly the fault of those who went from shop to shop buying as much as they could get their hands on – often domestics in the employ of the wealthy.

In parallel with the work of the Committee, the courts clamped down on hoarders and profiteers. On 18 January Mr and Mrs Levi, tailors of 5 Brunswick Street, Chorlton-on Medlock, appeared in court charged with hoarding food. They had no less than ten sacks of flour, 368 lb of sugar and 3 cwt of salt among a large stock of comestibles. They were fined £25, as was James Doherty Junior, a Smithfield Market trader, who was selling butter at four pence a pound above the regulation price.

When Saturday, 26 January arrived, the day of the factory workers' food strike, the turnout of 5,000 was far less than anticipated. Transport workers and most munitions workers reported to their place of employment as usual. Mr A.A. Purcell, after reading the strikers' manifesto to those who had gathered in Albert Square and calling for a just distribution of food, presented his demands at the Town Hall. Separate events in Openshaw and Trafford Park were also sparsely attended.

The immediate effect of the demonstrations, however, was an announcement by the Food Control Committee that meat would be added to the list of rationed foods; but it came with a warning that the allocations would amount to no more than half of what people had been used to. In fact the amount allocated was one shilling's worth of meat per household. Fortunately, the supply of rabbits began to improve at the end of January.

On 6 February the Food controller issued an amnesty to all hoarders, allowing them a week to turn over food. After that offenders could expect to be imprisoned.

The children's situation was helped by the fact that school meals were available for a few pence and free to those who could not afford it. This principle was extended on 7 February when the city's first communal kitchen opened at Barmouth Street, Openshaw. Every day except Sunday it served 2,000 meals. Soup was a penny-halfpenny a portion, meat and vegetable stew four pence, and milk pudding two pence. The scheme was such an immediate success that the Food Control Committee decided to extend it across the city, using Mayfield, Bradford and Moss Side public baths as central communal kitchens from where the food was sent to stations in each area. As the year progressed the need increased. In late August two more food kitchens were opened, amid much publicity, at Heyrod Street Lads' Club, Ancoats and Ashton Old Road, Clayton.

The new food allowances were announced in March: butter/margarine, four ounces, tea, one ounce and sugar, three ounces per person per week. The general reaction was unfavourable – in particular the meagre tea ration gave rise to widespread criticism, especially as tea was not rationed in either Liverpool or London.

In mid-March coal rationing was introduced in the city. It was already in operation in London. The end of the Easter holiday was marked by the introduction of early closing for all picture houses, theatres and places of entertainment. Even hotel dining rooms and restaurants were required to close by 10 pm. Fish and chip shops, already hard hit by shortages and increased prices, could not stay open beyond 9.30 pm.

Unfortunately rationing and price fixing did nothing for the hapless smoker. By mid-April there was a shortage of tobacco in the city. At the same time the number of rail routes available to civilians was further reduced, with routes to Bradford and a number of other Yorkshire cities cut.

On 13 June it was announced that two days hence strawberries would no longer be available to the public as growers would be obliged thereafter to supply them only to registered jam manufacturers. When this news broke hordes of people raced to Smithfield Market resulting in one of the swiftest markets in recent times. The precious fruit sold briskly at 2/- a pound and was all gone by 6.30 am.

In such circumstances it is hardly surprising that everyone wanted to join the 5,000 allotment holders in the city.

Every local newspaper immediately became a conduit for information and reminders to amateur growers. On 4 April one warned that the Food Production Department was gravely concerned that unless the ground was vigorously prepared within the next couple of weeks there would be a severe shortage of potatoes. This, readers were told, would be a calamity, as it was almost certain that the meat ration – introduced on 7 April – was to be further reduced. It warned that people should not assume that because potatoes were currently plentiful this would continue to be the case. The prediction about meat proved correct: on 5 May it was reduced to three pence worth of butcher's meat per person per week. Amateur growers – together with the farmers – clearly heeded the April warnings as the 1918 potato crop was at least twenty-five per cent more than that of 1917.

It was at the beginning of April that a new fear surfaced as rumours spread throughout the city: the food position, it was said, was so bad that Britain might be forced to end the war in order to avoid starvation. These fears were expressed in several local papers and there is no doubt that both the government and the city authorities believed that people should be made aware of the gravity of the situation. Many believed that the quality of the corn harvest would be decisive.

Rationing, however, did nothing to reduce discontent with the meat situation. There were numerous complaints that butchers were exploiting the fact that customers were tied to them in order sell them inferior meat. The butchers' spokesmen, of course, rejected this, protesting that they had been reduced to 'no more than the agents of the government for the retailing of meat'.

One butcher who certainly did seek to exploit the situation came to grief in June when he appeared before the Police Court. Not only did Richard Booker of Oxford

Road, Chorlton-cum-Hardy, order meat in excess of his entitlement: he sought to sell the excess at inflated prices. The Court regarded this as a grave offence which endangered the entire rationing system and fined him the enormous sum of £450.

Food was now the city's foremost concern: the availability of meat, the quality of the margarine and the nature of the fish on sale were the major topics of conversation. The brewers demonstrated their ability to respond to the changing situation and announced at the end of April that they were to produce a lighter and cheaper ale specifically for the needs of munitions workers and those in workshops. It was widely known as 'munition beer'.

Complaints about the poor quality of bread continued. The authorities responded that too much of it was being wasted while the consumers retorted that this was because it was often inedible. By trial and error it became generally accepted that it was far more tolerable when eaten with soup or toasted and regarded as a substitute for cake. It was in the latter form that many cafés sold it.

The Licensing Committee was receiving complaints from both police and public about the manner in which many landlords were responding to the shortage of beer and reduced opening. In early June, Sir Thomas Shann, chairman of the Committee, warned licensees against refusing to sell what supplies they had through the off-license – where it was cheaper – and especially against allowing favoured customers to drink behind closed doors after hours. Sir Thomas was clearly not a drinker, as he revealed by asserting that 'one pint of beer is enough for any man'.

Sir Thomas also warned landlords against 'the prevalent practice' of using unwashed glasses, which was on the increase now that pubs were opened for fewer hours. This was likely, he said, to lead to the transmission of tuberculosis – a major killer – syphilis and serious forms of diarrhoea.

The government was extremely concerned that shortage of labour on the land might make the food situation even worse. In 1917 large numbers of children had worked on farms during the holidays and once more the National Service Department appealed for 40,000 youngsters to help. They were paid at a rate of 4d an hour. It was hoped that this year more than the 200 Manchester Grammar School boys who took part in the scheme in 1917 would be involved. In late July one batch from the School went off to Fleet and a second to Peterborough, to live under canvas while flax stripping. In August further groups went potato picking in Ormskirk, Lincolnshire, Holbeach and Stoke Rochford. In total over 300 boys took part in these schemes while others worked on farms by individual arrangement.

Despite this the agricultural situation reached crisis point in early April when exhausted farm labourers in Cheshire rebelled. They went on strike, demanding an end to the inordinate length of their working week, calling to have Saturday afternoon and Sunday off. The National Farmers' Union, representing the farmers, was so concerned about the mood of the men that it telegraphed the Prime Minister, asking for his help to get the men back to work.

The burden of feeding families in such difficult circumstance fell largely on women, many of whom were involved in performing what traditionally had been men's jobs. The prevalence of women in industry was now evident everywhere. In many workshops more than half the workers were women and in some there was hardly a man to be seen. In one modern chain factory in the city the number of workers doubled during the war and the percentage of women increased from twenty-seven to fifty-five. A textile machinery manufacturer that employed only four female typists in 1914 had 750 women workers by 1918. One of the biggest employers in the city, which employed 833 women before the war, had over 3,000 by its end. By June 1918 three large armaments factories employed 20,000 women, sixty per cent of them released from the cotton industry. In Lancashire alone, 150,000 women were employed in engineering work connected with the war.

Like their male counterparts, women's lives were bedevilled by the relentless upward trend in the price of essentials, which constantly reduced the real value of wages and locked them into an endless round of conflict with employers. However, it was those at the opposite extreme, the new aristocracy of affluent labour, who were attracting public interest. Among these fortunate ones were the engineers: by May 1918 the average male engineering worker was earning from £3 to £4 a week and his female counterpart between £2 10s 0d and £3. This was reflected in the increasing number of people able to open deposits with the Manchester Savings Bank, the decline in the use of pawnbrokers and the reports of the Charity Organisation Association.

Others, like those in the cotton industry, were suffering great hardship. After a meeting at the Victoria Hotel, all the cotton unions simultaneously applied for a thirty per cent pay rise. The employers granted twenty-five per cent. But this was not the end of conflict in the industry. When the Cotton Control Board announced that it was about to discontinue the programme of rolling unemployment – whereby workers were periodically laid off on a rota basis – the unions immediately made it clear that any attempt to force continuous unemployment on any of its members would result in an all-out strike.

On 8 August, after 1,500 employees of the city council had gone on strike, the authority awarded paviors, flaggers and certain other municipal workers, a twelve and a half per cent bonus for the duration of the war and a £1 rise. But Manchester street cleaners and rubbish collectors remained on strike and were soon joined by their counterparts in Salford. By 13 August the newspapers were complaining that both cities were becoming 'disagreeably dirty' as 'the filth accumulates and the house-fly thrives'. Many hotels were taking measures to burn whatever they could incinerate, while at Smithfield Market the stallholders were doing their best to dispose of waste but it nevertheless accumulated on the city streets, where rubbish bins were overflowing. To make matters worse, the weather was unusually warm.

As the dispute dragged on the Corporation tried to draft in men to launch a clean-up. This served only to arouse the ire of Manchester and District Branch of the Discharged and Demobilised Soldiers, which issued an angry statement that 'their members will never be used as strike breakers'. Eventually, after a day and night of continuous negotiation, the men went back to work, having won a bonus of 16/- a week and the promise of arbitration on their claim for a twelve and a half per cent rise. Unusually, the local newspapers were unanimous in support of the workers' cause and their strike action.

Industrial discontent was by no means confined to Manchester, as all over the country a combination of war weariness, suppressed grievances and a growing resentment at what many workers saw as the war being used as a pretext for exploitation, led to a plethora of strikes. All public transport in London was at a standstill and 10,000 building workers in Dublin were also on strike.

On 24 August hundreds of striking Co-Operative Wholesale Society workers marched through the city. The Company's biscuit works in Crumpsall, which employed 700 girls and young women, stood empty. The public feared that the action might spread to the Society's shops, with a disastrous effect on food supply. Two days later the strike did spread when another 900 workers in the wholesale section at Middleton joined the action.

Perhaps the most illuminating strike is one that received little attention at the time and involved no great public demonstrations. In early September 200 attendants – both nurses and keepers – at Prestwich Asylum, after months of negotiation, went on strike. The Asylum Attendants Union nevertheless allowed some of its members to remain at work to care for the aged and infirm. Some staff regularly worked eighty hours a week, but the Board would neither consider their grievances nor accept arbitration. The maximum wage was £40 a year. After a meeting of the Board on 5 September, the asylum workers agreed to return to work. Their new terms were never revealed.

On 9 September 18,000 cotton spinners went on strike and thereby make a total of 300,000 workers idle, while disrupting the production of many materials vital to the war effort. By 16 September there were sixteen million spindles idle. This action was in clear defiance of the union's officials and incurred the real risk that the government would declare the strike illegal and thus prevent the workers from receiving strike pay. On the same day the bulk of the CWS workers returned to work.

It was not until 23 September that the cotton workers went back to work on the promise of arbitration. Two days later the railway strike reached Manchester, when the men rejected a proposed 5/- rise, demanding an additional 5/-. On the same day the Manchester District Council of the Associated Society of Locomotive Engineers, Firemen and Cleaners declared an immediate strike. Their president, Councillor Jackson of Patricroft, said his men would continue to move troops, hospital and stock trains in relation to troops, but nothing else. The feeling in the city, even among those who were generally sympathetic to labour, was hostile and many were indignant in that they felt the railway men had received wartime rises beyond any other group of workers. Fortunately, the strike was resolved the following day and the men immediately returned to work.

Even the police were not immune to the contagion of industrial action and, unusually, their employers supported them. The city's Watch Committee, accompanied by the Chief Constable, Mr Peacock, went to London in early October to petition the Home Secretary on behalf of the Manchester branch of the Union of Police and Prison Officials, which was demanding immediate recognition of their union and a hundred per cent increase on pre-war pay. Pre-war pay was 28/- on appointment, rising to 40/- after twenty years' service.

Within a week the police accepted a war bonus of 12/- a week and an additional 2/6 a week for each child of school age.

Many of those who won pay rises found that they were immediately offset by new demands on their resources. By July there were 2,400 men of the Manchester Regiment prisoners of war in Germany and dependent on the War Comforts Committee and the efforts of their families for much of their food and all of their clothing. The Committee sent two sets of clothes to each man per year and food parcels. The girls of the Manchester High

School took the men to their hearts and raised money for them, presenting it to the Lord Mayor on their speech day. One of the beneficiaries was Private Martin Jennings, who wrote to his wife in Middleton from his camp in Limburg: 'I am in the best of health. The only thing I am looking forward to now is a parcel every week and a few cough drops, as the weather out here is very cold. They give us a little work every day and it passes the time away.'

The news from the front was depressing. In spring the Germans launched a great offensive on the Western Front, sweeping all before them and threatening to overwhelm the Allies. For the first time since the early months of war, military defeat threatened.

Oppressed by military defeats, shortages, worry, long working hours and incessant government demands for greater effort, people inevitably turned their anger on those who seemed to be shirking their duty. Foremost among the enemies of the cause were those who would not fight.

Many Manchester conscientious objectors were held in Knutsford Prison, where they attracted a great deal of hostile attention. As they returned from their walk one Sunday evening in January a crowd, lying in wait, attacked them. The 'conscies', however, were prepared and having armed themselves with sticks, retaliated. The police eventually broke up the disturbance but not before several men were injured, notably a wounded soldier who had taken no part in events but was hit by a stone.

Violence reoccurred later in the year as a result of which Knutsford Police Court was crammed on 17 May to hear the case of ten young men charged with a breach of the peace during a demonstration against the conscies, whose presence in the town was increasingly resented. The feeling against them was such that the town's Tradesmen's Association paid for the defence of the men accused of attacking them in Canute Place and then chasing them back to the prison where what the police described as 'a riot' took place. The magistrate bound over the men for six months.

Antagonism against 'shirkers' became rabid and showed itself clearly in April at the trial of George Anderson, a Manchester United player, who was accused of defrauding people who had placed bets on matches in which he was involved. What really antagonised court and public, however, was the fact that Anderson had originally been unaccountably rejected for the army on the grounds that he was unfit but, having recently been re-examined, was found to be in the highest category of physical fitness. Mr Justice Slater, describing his behaviour as 'disgusting and disgraceful', sent him down for four months.

Events in Ireland were also fuelling resentment against Manchester's large Irish population. Nationalist feeling in Ireland was increasingly associated with opposition to the introduction of conscription there, as growing numbers of nationalists took the anti-conscription pledge.

In April 1918 the term 'war weariness' first appeared in the local press. One paper said that exhaustion was 'everywhere apparent'. It was also evident in the physical environment. The shortage of paint, for instance, meant that public buildings and private homes all appeared dingy and down at heel. Even Belle Vue Gardens, for so long a delight of colour, now spoke of long neglect.

Speaking of the August Bank Holiday, one local writer captured the atmosphere in the city perfectly. 'The term pleasure-seeker,' he wrote, 'can hardly with justice be applied to the holiday-makers of today, pleasure in the sense which we interpreted it five years ago seems a thing so unobtainable that people have ceased to pursue it and are content to seek out any recreation, to seize opportunities for physical recuperation and forgetfulness for a day of the pressing problems of the hour. The demeanour of the crowds parading the Manchester streets has noticeably altered. One was struck by the absence of the youthful element...with youth also has gone much of the effervescence, the heedless gaiety...which in the old days gave such a marked character to bank holiday crowds. There are not many temptations to hilarity when every street and every congregation of mankind are clothed with the blue uniforms of crippled and wounded men. And laughter is apt to die away when a Red Cross ambulance glides softly past. The shadows of the war are reflected also in the apparel of the people one met today. We have heard a great deal about the fabulous sums spent by artisans and women workers in personal decoration, but there was little indication of this form of extravagance in Manchester. Everywhere sober tints prevailed: the feminine element showed a marked preference for the subdued and the male popinjay has apparently suffered complete extinction – a real subject for regret as he added such mirth to all ages.'

News from the front certainly did nothing to raise spirits at home. In February the Manchesters were holding out against vastly superior forces at what was known as Manchester Hill, a redoubt west of St Quentin. The CO of the 16th Manchesters (1st City), Lieutenant Colonel Elstrob, sent a message to HQ, telling his superiors that 'here we fight and here we die'. His final communication said that he, like his few surviving men, was wounded but determined to fight to the end. Eventually they were overwhelmed

Lieutenant Colonel Elstrob.

Manchester Hill circled.

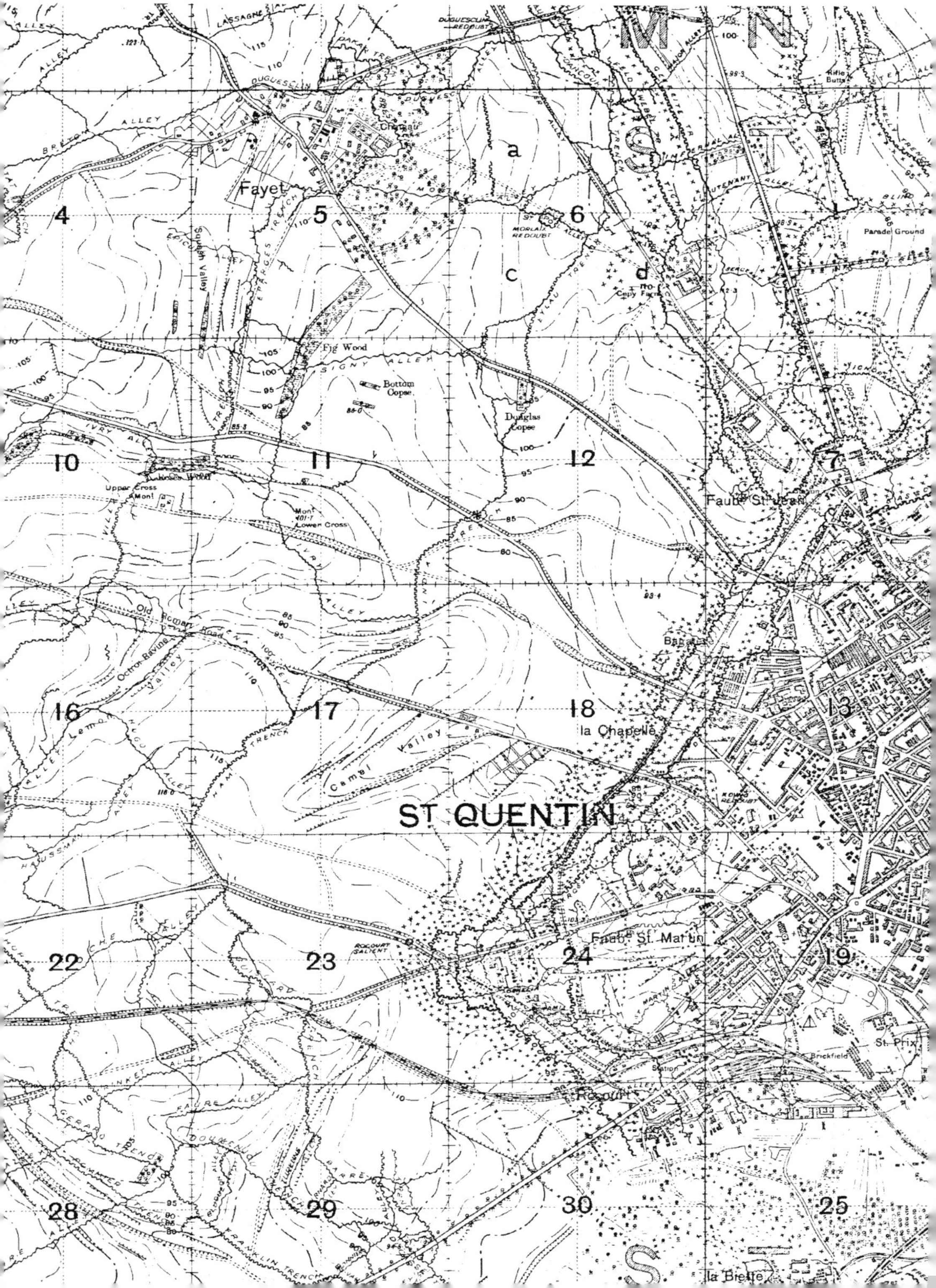
Fayet
Fig Wood
Bottom Copse
Douglas Copse
Upper Cross Mont
Mont 101·7 Lower Cross
Old Roman Road
Octroi Ravine
Camel Valley
la Chapelle
Faub. St Jean
Faub. St Martin
ST QUENTIN
Rocourt
Station
Brickfield
St. Prix
Parade Ground
Rifle Butts
Cepy Farm
Squash Valley
Morlaix Redoubt
Duguesclin Redoubt
Rocourt Salient
Signy Alley
Ivry Alley
Lassagne
Faure Alley
Franklin Trench
Haussman
la Biette
a
c
d
4
5
6
7
10
11
12
13
16
17
18
19
22
23
24
25
28
29
30

The town of St Quentin in 1917. The cathedral dominated the area, which by 1918, had been reduced to a shadow of its former splendour. Taylor Library

Overwhelming concentrations of German troops were assembled in St Quentin prior to their attack on the morning of 21 March 1918. Taylor Library

by four German divisions. The 16th Manchesters had defended Manchester Hill to the last. In a subsequent attempt to retake the hill 17th Manchesters were also destroyed as a fighting force.

The gallantry of the men briefly united the city. Bishop Welldon spoke for all when he expressed his admiration for the men's heroism.

The city did, however, get several boosts during this black period. On 24 June the King of the Belgians awarded Mrs J. Mathewson Watson the Medaille de la Reine Elizabeth in recognition of the Manchester woman's 'kind help and valuable assistance' to both soldiers and refugees.

On 16 July a further much-needed shaft of joy broke through the gloom that enveloped the city. As a child growing in Levenshulme, Joe Carley remembers that school ended early that day so the children could line the route. Cheers echoed round the streets as the Americans disembarked at Salford Docks and marched into Manchester across the New Bailey Bridge, greeted all the way by ecstatic crowds, every second one flourishing the Stars and Stripes. These fresh youths represented deliverance from the drudgery of an interminable ordeal. The Lord Mayor was waiting in Albert Square, beneath the Old Glory fluttering from the Town Hall, to receive them officially. They then marched, visibly buoyed by the warmth of their reception, to Belle Vue. Joe remembers that they left their regimental mascot, a goat, there, where it could be seen for many years. The press was unanimous: the crowd's 'enthusiasm was unceasing and boundless and Manchester has never witnessed such rousing and inspiring scenes. From start to finish it was one long triumphant progress.'

And at last, the news from the front was improving. In late July all the local newspapers told their readers that the Germans were in retreat to the east of Paris. By early August they had fallen back across the Aisne. Then, just as the tide was turning in

Belle Vue, where the American troops' mascot, a goat, could be seen for years after the war.
Mark Flynn Postcards

favour of the Allies, a new, seemingly unstoppable engine of death swept though the city.

By June 1918 influenza was widespread throughout Manchester, especially in schools. The School Medical Officer, Dr Alexander Brown Ritchie, was so concerned that he closed two schools in Chorlton-on-Medlock to prevent further contagion. He did, however, assure the public that the ailment was no different from that which was common during some winters; it was not a 'new malady', he said, as some seemed to believe. What was unusual, however, was the extent of the condition, which had already seriously reduced the number of people at work in factories and offices.

As the summer progressed the epidemic tightened its grip on the city. Many warehouses were clogged up with goods for lack of men to move them and so many tram workers were absent though illness – 220 on 27 June – that forty trams were cancelled that day and seventy a few days later.

On 30 June the first deaths were reported – two in Heywood. The toll mounted daily. By July every part of the city was affected, more schools were closed and doctors – of which there was a severe shortage – were 'reaching breaking point', while 'the depletion of all public services involves serious inconvenience and delay in all areas of city life'.

Within the month the disease had attained Biblical proportions and one local newspaper reported that 'hardly a household seems to have been spared its pestilential breath and mountains of work are being left undone as it cuts great swathes through factories and warehouses'. In the first week of July the disease claimed seventy lives in

The retreating German army in 1918.

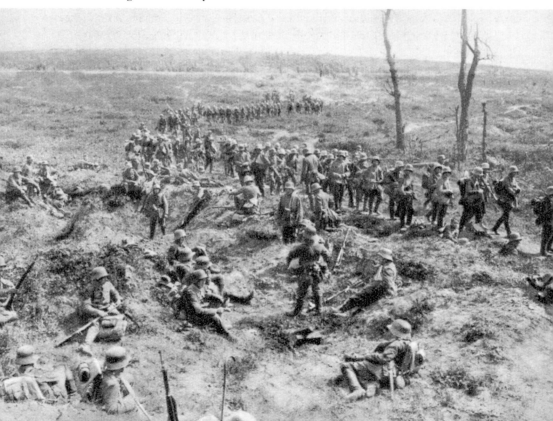

the city and it was clear that it was far more virulent than anyone had realized. Though the situation on the trams was improving – only seventeen per cent of staff were absent – as drivers and conductors gradually returned to work, many more factories and warehouses were hit to such an extent that they were unable to stay open. It seemed that at this stage of its development the disease was attacking many domestic servants and congregations at churches and synagogues were significantly reduced.

In the week up to 15 July, influenza killed 119 people, with a further fifty-nine deaths attributed to pneumonia. One of the victims was John Johnson of Ogden Street, Hulme. He was 7 years old.

There was a lull until October, when, as news of German collapse and retreat was coming through daily, the 'flu once more came to the fore. This time it was more virulent than ever. It swept through schools so rapidly that soon one in ten children was affected. Within a week fourteen schools closed and most people in the city centre were wearing face masks, believed to prevent the spread of the infection.

The 'worst is over', Lloyd George confidently told the people of Manchester on his visit to the city on 10 September. He was referring to the war but in the event, the city almost claimed his life.

On his arrival at the Town Hall at 11.20 am the Prime Minister was received like the conquering hero. His wife and the Lady Mayoress, each bearing an enormous bouquet, preceded him up the steps and past the statues of Jeule and Dalton, two of the city's greatest scientific pioneers. An hour later he raised his silk hat to the cheering crowd in Albert Square and his white hair fluttered in the cool breeze. No sooner had the procession reached Princess Street than the rain fell. The length of Portland Street and Oxford Street to the Hippodrome was lined with cheering crowds showing no evidence of war weariness. His reception in the hall was overwhelming and he appeared moved by its warmth.

In conferring the freedom of the city, the Lord Mayor told him that 'We are proud of the fact that you are the first Manchester man who has become Prime Minister.' The same day the local papers reported significant American advances in the St Mihiel sector, near Metz, and the capture of over 13,000 German prisoners.

But instead of leaving for Blackpool, as scheduled, the following day the Prime Minister was confined to bed in the in Town Hall as a result of what the papers described as 'a chill'. Outside the rain fell relentlessly in what was the city's wettest September for decades.

It was not until 18 September that the Prime Minister actually left the Town Hall, appearing at the Lloyd Street entrance, swathed in scarves and a heavy overcoat, looking pale and wearing a respirator as he followed his doctor's order to take some fresh air. Three days later he took his subdued leave from Exchange Station without any prior publicity.

Lloyd George's prediction, however, was coming true. The headline in the *Manchester Evening News* for Saturday, 12 October proclaimed the 'Beginning of the End'. For the first time the paper mentioned that the Germans were seeking peace terms – though the government seemed to treat this with contempt, dismissing it as a cynical ruse.

Five days later the Allies entered Lille and Ostend. The enormous number of prisoners taken suggested that German morale was collapsing. In early November news of the German naval mutiny at Kiel reached Manchester.

On 9 November the local papers all got it wrong – telling readers that the armistice would take effect at 11 am on 10 November. When the correct information appeared the following day, it was printed next to a long list of local men killed or gone missing over the week end. These were among the last Manchester men to lose their lives during the war. One was Lance Corporal F. Coote of 18 Railway Street, Gorton, his parents' third son to make the supreme sacrifice. He had served in Egypt, the Dardanelles and France.

The following day the Town Hall bells rang out and flags fluttered from every building. A wounded Tommy threw his crutch into the air and hopped a one-legged jig. Bells pealed, fireworks fizzed, ships' sirens hooted while thousands wept. Across the city, from Clayton to Chorlton, from Bradford to Benchill, workers downed tools, discarded their aprons and took to the streets. Girls left their shops, offices and sewing machines and burst like starlings onto the streets, hugging and kissing every soldier and sailor in sight.

Yelling newspaper boys handed out a special edition of the *Manchester Evening News* while total strangers linked arms and danced in a prancing mob towards Albert Square, where they fed into an enormous crowd singing God Save the King. From the steps of the town hall the new Lord Mayor, John Makeague, hushed the crowd to silence and announced to a great roar that the following day was to be a holiday. But the city had

The armistice is signed on 11 November 1918 between the French, English and Germans in a railway carriage in woods at Compiègne.

pre-empted his announcement and hardly a shop, office or factory was open. Telephone switchboards were silent, trains and trams stood idle and cabs were nowhere to be seen.

On Market Street a party of wounded American soldiers half-marched, half-limped, flourishing an enormous Stars and Stripes. On the opposite pavement four women in black, carrying wreathes, made no attempt to staunch the tears that glistened on their faces.

By midday the centre of the city was rapidly filling up as women and girls flooded in from all points of the compass, most walking or hitching rides on horse-drawn vehicles. As darkness drew on the city was a ball of light in the winter landscape, blackout restrictions forgotten, the streets and shops aglow with lights long dimmed. The Lord Mayor conducted the crowds in singing God Save the King. Some older people looked on indulgently, while strangers linked onto each other and sang 'Are We Downhearted?'

But under the shadow of the Cathedral there were bowed heads. Young men and women mingled with the old and middle aged who formed a constant stream of people drawn instinctively to the oldest building in the city. They passed through its great doors and sat in the dimness, illuminated only by a few candles.

One Commonwealth serviceman buried in Southern Cemetery.

That evening every bar and restaurant, all the music halls and picture palaces hummed with the glee of intoxicated crowds. There was an outbreak of impromptu speech making, prolonged cheering and the endless, exhilarated singing of patriotic songs. Exuberant carousers wandered aimlessly about the city centre.

By the end of Tuesday, 12 November, it seemed that the excitement had died down, as the single great surge of exhilaration had drained those exhausted by long years of labour, worry and Spartan living.

There were others, who had not joined in the riotous celebrations. As one local newspaper put it, 'There were those who regarded these world-stirring events as a matter of solemn significance to be fittingly celebrated by quiet thankfulness or by prayer and thanksgiving at home.'

But this was not the end of the dying. Before December 'flu was again rampant and every school in the city was closed. In November and December alone it claimed 1,580 lives.

During the war 4,776 men died serving in the Manchester Pals' battalions and the death toll among the whole regiment was 13,000; while the Lancashire Fusiliers, recruited from areas north of Manchester and Salford, lost 13,600. It is estimated that

Memorial to the men of 7th Manchesters, Whitworth Park.

IN GLORIOUS MEMORY OF ALL RANKS OF THE 7TH MANCHESTER WHO GAVE THEIR LIVES FOR THEIR COUNTRY 1914 — 1918

Memorial to the dead of the Great War, Southern Cemetery.

the Manchester and Salford area lost more than 22,000 men killed and 55,000 casualties. In some way every family was touched. A post war survey found that one in eight widows died within twelve months of their husband's death.

Emma Pollitt's uncle Fred – he of the egg and bacon pies – returned from the war physically uninjured. He never spoke of his experiences. Edith Parker's brother, Charles, died near the end of the war. Fifty years later, with her last breath, she called his name.

For many, like these soldiers in a Rusholme hospital, the war did not end in 1918.
Rusholme Archives

Index

Abbey Hay, 30–1, 67
Accrington, 11
Albert Hall, 18, 40
Albert Square, 32, 71, 75–6, 85, 87–8
Aliens, 28, 31
Alderley Edge, 9
Allotments, 64–5, 77
Americans, 29, 69, 85, 87, 89
Angel Meadow, 26
Ancoats, 9, 29, 64, 77
Ardwick, 13, 20, 30–1, 33, 54, 56
Army pay, 16–18, 41
Ashton-under-Lyne, 11, 61
AVRO, 37

Bantams, Bob's, 19
Belgium, 13, 15, 20, 29, 36
Belle Vue, 14, 18, 85
Beer, 39, 43, 62, 71, 74, 78
BEF (British Expeditionary Force), 13
Beswick, 31
Bigamy, 62
Black market, 46
Blackout, 36, 48–9, 89
Bradford (Manchester), 30–1, 39, 76–7, 88
Brewers, 43, 62, 74, 78
Broughton, Higher, 25
British Workers' League, 69–70
Builders, 22, 24, 80
Burlington Street Barracks, 14

Canals, 8–9, 13, 29, 36, 51, 61
Carters, 41, 67
Casualties, 13, 23, 25, 28, 31, 34, 57–9, 91
Cavell, Edith, 29
Charter Street, 25
Charity, 24, 35, 44, 51, 79
Cheetham Hill, 13, 41
Chetham's School, 10, 35
Cheadle, 22
Chief Constable, 27, 31, 37, 44, 75, 80
Children, 9, 11, 13, 18, 20, 24–9, 35, 46, 48–51, 53, 56, 62–5, 74, 76, 78, 80, 85, 87

Chorlton-cum-Hardy, 41, 78, 88
Chorlton-on-Medlock, 41, 76, 86
City Corporation, 16, 18, 22, 49, 64, 79
Clayton, 30–1, 61, 77, 88
Commerce, 9, 27
Conscientious Objectors, 45, 53–4, 81
Conscription, 33, 52–5, 66, 81
Co-Operative Wholesale Society (CWS), 67, 80
Coroner, 36, 74
Consumption, 10, 47
Cotton industry, 8, 11, 21–2, 24, 26, 51, 61, 66–7, 79–80
Court, Assize, 50, 62
Court, Police, 11, 15, 33, 39, 41–2, 47, 51, 54, 64, 68, 71, 77–8, 81
Crime, 50, 62

Derby, Earl of (Edward George Villiers Stanley, 17th Earl of Derby), 17, 33, 40, 44
Distress Committee, 21
Dockers, 9, 11, 21, 29, 41, 51, 67, 85
Didsbury, 19
Disabled, 82
Drink, 40, 42–3, 55–6, 62, 78

Electricity, 9, 13, 22, 41, 71
Engineering, 8–9, 21, 37, 49, 51, 79
Entertainment, 39, 46, 66, 77
Exhibition Hall, 14, 79

Food, 8, 21–2, 26, 40–2, 46–9, 53, 62–6, 69, 72–8, 80
Food Controller, 48, 62, 76
Flag days, 52
Flying Corps, Royal, 37

Gas, 8–9, 31, 35, 41, 49, 61
Germans, 12–13, 15, 21, 25–31, 35–6, 45, 63, 69, 80–1, 84–8
George V, King, 42, 70
George, Lloyd, 37–42, 87

Gorton, 12, 20, 30, 37-39, 41, 67, 75, 88
Grammar School, Manchester, 10, 78
Great Western Street, 8
Grocers, 12, 40, 46–8, 64–5, 74, 76
Greeks, 28

Hartlepool, 28–9
Heaton Park, 14–15, 19, 44–7, 52, 71
Hoarders, 65, 76
Hollingworth Camp, 14–15
Hooley Hill Rubber and Chemical Works, 61
Hospitals, 23–4, 33–6, 44, 51, 55, 61, 64, 71–2, 80, 92
Housing, 41
Hungarians, 28

Influenza, 86–7
Internment, 28
Ireland/Irish, 11, 15, 26, 45, 56, 64, 69, 81

Kitchener, Lord (Secretary of State for War), 16, 18, 32, 34, 42, 45, 58–9
Knockaloe Camp, 28
Knutsford, 81

Lancashire Cricket Ground, 35
Lancashire Fusiliers, 10, 12, 18, 19
Landlords, 41, 55, 66, 78
Levenshulme, 35, 41, 85
Licensing Laws, 42–3, 55, 78
Lusitania, 29

Manchester City FC, 39
Manchester Evening News, 11, 13, 22, 25, 42, 59, 87–8
Manchester Guardian, 13, 32
Manchester Regiment, 13, 17, 25, 45, 80
Manchester United FC, 39, 81
McCabe, Daniel, (Lord Mayor), 16, 18, 20, 75
Medical examinations, 15, 18, 52–5

Middle Class, 9, 17, 22, 24, 35, 48, 56, 63, 66
Midland Hotel, 28, 37–9
Miles Platting, 71
Military Service Act, 52, 54
Milton Hall, 47
Mission, Wood Street, 74
Morale, civilian, 62, 69
Moss Side, 41, 65, 76
Munitions, 22, 33, 37–9, 43–4, 48, 50–1, 68–9, 71, 75–6, 78
Music halls, 39–40, 51, 53, 66, 89

National Service League, 19
Newton Heath, 37
Nursing, Queen Alexandra's Imperial Military Nursing Service, 36
Nurses, 24, 29, 35–6, 72, 80

Officer Training Corps, 10
Oldham Road, 14, 29–31
Old Trafford, 10, 25, 28, 39, 42, 71

Pacifists, 69–70
Pals Battalions, 17–18, 34, 45, 58–9, 90
Parks Department, 47
Piccadilly, 14, 31
Picture halls, 39, 47, 60, 77, 89
Police, 28, 30–1, 50–1, 54–5, 67–70, 74, 78, 80–1
Prestwich, 34, 80
Prices, 12, 21–2, 26, 40–1, 46–8, 50–1, 60, 62, 64–6, 68–9, 72–4, 76–9
Prisons, 37, 56, 80–1
Prohibitionists, 55
Profiteers, 65, 76
POWs (Prisoners of War), 80, 87–8
Port of Manchester (Salford Docks), 9, 27
Public houses, 12, 55

Queuing, 18, 63–4, 74

Race Course, Manchester (Castle Irwell), 39
Railway Stations, 9, 13, 18, 23, 27–8, 30, 60, 69, 87

Railways, 8, 20–1, 25, 46, 50–1, 61–2, 86, 88
Rationing, 63, 76–7
Recruitment, 17–18, 29, 31–2, 55–7
Red Cross, 16, 20, 23–4, 33–4, 52, 72, 82
Refugees, 16, 20, 22, 27, 85
Relief Committee, 16
Rent and Mortgage interest (War Restrictions) Bill, 41
Rents, 41, 66
Reserves, 18
Retailers Traders' Association, 48, 55
Rusholme, 30–1, 92

Sailors, 69, 88
Salford, 10, 13, 22, 28–9, 35, 42, 47, 50–1, 54–6, 65, 69, 76, 79, 85, 90–1
Savings Bank, Manchester, 79
Savings, War, 48, 51
School, Manchester High, 80–1
Schools, 9–10, 13, 17, 24–5, 34–5, 49–51, 56, 71, 76, 78, 80–1, 85–7, 90
Scott, CP, 13
Separation allowance, 62
Serbian Relief Fund, 27
Servants, domestic, 87
Shirkers, 53, 56, 81
Shop stewards, 67
Shudehill, 13, 43, 47, 72
Smedhurst, Alderman Thomas, (Lord Mayor), 48
Smithfield Market, 43, 47, 64, 72, 76–7, 79
Soldiers, 11, 14, 16–17, 23–6, 29–31, 35, 41–2, 45, 51, 52–5, 62, 64, 69–72, 79, 81, 85, 88–9, 92
Somme, Battle of, 18, 45, 57–8
Special constables, 15, 30–1, 55
Stephenson Square, 69–70
Stockport Road, 35, 37, 41, 55
Stretford, 27
Strikes, 11, 29, 39, 41, 51, 66–8, 76, 78–80
Summer Time Act, 49

Teachers, 49–50, 56
Temperance Society, 42

Tenants' Association, 41
Tenants' Defence Committee, 66
Territorial Army, 9–10, 12, 14–18
Theatres, 39, 77
Thordis, the, 27
Tobacco, 35, 66, 77
Town Hall, 14, 18, 28, 31–4, 39, 48, 67, 75–6, 85, 87–8
Trade and Labour Council, 22
Trafford Park, 21, 29, 76
Tramps, 37
Trams, 8, 13, 27, 36–7, 50, 56, 63, 67–8, 86–7, 89
Tribunals, appeal, 52–4
Tuberculosis, 78
Turks, 28

Unemployment, 20, 22, 67, 79
University, Manchester, 10, 13, 17

VAD, (Voluntary Aid Detachment), 35

Wages, 14, 16, 21–2, 39, 41, 50–1, 66, 69, 79–80
War Problems Committee, Manchester and Salford, 47–8
Weariness, war, 69, 79, 81, 87
Whalley Range, 36
White City, 14
Whitworth Street, 17, 23, 24, 35, 55, 71
Wilmslow, 9
Women's Army Auxiliary Corps, 35
Women's Defence Relief Corps, 35
Women's Emergency Corps, 35
Women's Hospital Corps, 35
Women's National service Corps, 35
Women's War Interests Committee, 48, 50
Wounded soldiers, 16, 23–5, 29–30, 35, 52, 70–2, 81–2, 88–9

YMCA, 95

Zeppelins, 28, 48–9